No Illusions

Through the Looking Glass

Jackie Davis Allen

inner child press, ltd.

Credits

Author
Jackie Davis Allen

Editor
hulya n. yılmaz, Ph.D.

Cover Art
Jackie Davis Allen

Cover Design
William S. Peters Sr.
inner child press, ltd.

General Information

No Illusions

Author: Jackie Davis Allen

1st Edition: 2019

This Publishing is protected under Copyright Law as a "Collection". All rights for all submissions are retained by the Individual Author and or Artist. No part of this Publishing may be Reproduced, Transferred in any manner without the prior **WRITTEN CONSENT** of the "Material Owner" or its Representative, Inner Child Press. Any such violation infringes upon the Creative and Intellectual Property of the Owner, pursuant to International and Federal Copyright Law. Any queries pertaining to this "Collection" should be addressed to Publisher of Record.

Publisher Information:
1st Edition: Inner Child Press
intouch@innerchildpress.com
www.innerchildpress.com

This Collection is protected under U.S. and International Copyright Laws

Copyright © 2019: Jackie Davis Allen

ISBN-13: 978-1-970020-69-4 (inner child press, ltd.)

$ 24.95

For All Those Who Have a Story to Tell

Table of Contents

Acknowledgements   *xvii*
Preface   *xix*
Foreword   *xxi*
Introduction   *xxiii*

The Poetic and Prosaic Narrative

You Might Be Surprised	3
Dreaming	4
In Those Days	5
Life Is a Tapestry	6
Me, as a Child	7
And, It Came to Pass	8
Determination	14
I Still Remember	15
so old, the story	17
Indian Summer	18
Moving Day	19
Looking Back	22
A Most Memorable Day	23
Heart-of-Gold	25
Bee-Balm Garden	26
All the Way	27
Time	28
of a moment left wanting	29
Fancy the Concept	30
Moment of Brilliance	31

Table of Contents... *continued*

While the Candles Burn	32
Poesy	33
Who Am I?	34
Winter's Might	35
Midnight Prayers	36
Revisiting the Scene	37
Her Royal Inadequacy	41
Window of Expectation	42
Sitting on the Fence	43
Searching for the Magic	44
Dinner on the Ground	45
Observation	46
Confessional	47
The Child	48
My Mother's Mother	49
Forever	50
Fearfully Formed	51
Garden of Grace	52
The Thief	53
Delirious	54
Dawn	55
Hiding in Plain Sight	56
Heart-Strings	59
The Color of Fear	60
Grace	61
After the Rainfall	62
On the Path Again	63
Diary of My Discontent	64
First Place	66

Table of Contents ... *continued*

Seeds	67
Summer-Rose	68
My Favorite Spot	69
Winter's Solace	70
A Picturesque Scene	71
Lack of Communication	72
This Morning	73
Garden-Song	74
Of a Time Past	75
Time's Benevolent Grace	77
The Umbrella	78
Someone Is Watching	79
Mistreated	80
Good Day	81
The Golden Ones	83
On the Right Path	84
At My Desk	85
Old Red Top	86
The Snows of Tomorrow	87
A Summer-Morning	88
sibling rivalry	90
I Am My Mother's Daughter	91
A Taste of Orange	94
The Midnight-Hour	95
A Fine Shade of Pink	97
The Mystery Behind the Doors	98
A Daughter of Appalachia	99
Whimsy	102
Peace, an Elusive Truce	103

Table of Contents . . . *continued*

Between Friends, Neighbors	104
The Idiom of the Day	105
The Purloined Papers	106
Behind the Door	114
Nightmare	115
Think You upon This!	117
Spirit-Song	118
Where There Is a Will . . .	119
in the blink of an eye	120
Tapestry	121
autumn's chill	122
O Lord, Have Mercy!	123
Lonely	125
One of a Kind	126
A Turn in the Road	127
Garden of Dreams	128
Revision Quest	129
The Winter of His Age	130
On the Other Hand	131
Happy Birthday to Me	132
The Colors We Wear	133
Promises, Colors and Coupons	137
Hope	140
Wishful Thinking	141
First Love	142
The Night-Visitors	143
Christmas Eve	147
The Night Before Last	148
Intercession	149

Table of Contents... *continued*

A Night Filled with Choices	150
House on the Hill	151
The Survivors	152
Reflections	153
A Breakthrough	156
At My Window	157
Embracing the Gift	158
Birds of a Different Feather	159
contemplation	160
Chasing Sleep	161
Time for Prayer	162
Here I Am	164
A New Day Is Here	166
Consideration	167
Ode to Never-More	168
God Only Knows	170
clueless	171
Always	172
The Thread Unraveled	173
The Matchmaking Snafu	174
Milking Time	177
Of Life and Loss	179
Chimera	180
Sunrise	182
Adjustments	183
interlude	184
farewell	185
Beyond Definition	186
Aching	187

Table of Contents ... *continued*

Poetic Elixir	188
Are You Still There?	189
Some Dreams Do Come True	190
No Need for Dialogue	191
Charting the Course	192
Like India-Ink	193
the ocean	194
indite	195
A Feather in Her Hat?	196
Videos, Redactions and Lies	197
Intentions	198
First Edition	199
Hungry	200
First Grade: A Troubling Beginning	201
Facing the Brick Wall	205
Callie Mae's Story	206
A Glimpse of Truth	214
Pleading Courage	215
May I Awaken to a Better Day	216
Crones, Weeds and an Exorcism	217
Full Circle	223
rain-dance, rain-song	224
well done	225
Once Again	226
Tongue-in-Cheek	227
The Dream	228
with eyes wide open	229
Life's Breath	230
The Weather's Eye	231

Table of Contents... *continued*

What He Said	232
A Reminder	233
Someone Is at the Door	234
Time Has Lost All Meaning	235
Not Yet Spring	236
Buried Treasure	237
Trajectory	238
A Vision Beyond the Mountains	239
Building Up, Tearing Down	244
Sweet Molly	246
Waiting for Winter	247
More than Meets the Eye	248
Caught Up	249
Determined	250
Novel	251
In Step with Fashion	252
Patience	253
So Many Questions	254
Battle-Weary	255
Contagious	256
a million stars in the sky	257
This Side of Heaven	258
Incomprehensible	259
Between Darkness and Dawn	260
Say, It Isn't So!	261
Alas! I Am the Mother	262
In My Dreams	263
Something	264
What to Do?	265

Table of Contents... *continued*

A Song of Lamentation and Hope	266
They Begged for More	267
fissures of futility	268
An Appalachian Saga	269
One Man's Story	274
The Way It Used to Be	275
A Party to Attend	278
Grace, Sweet Grace	279
Innocence Lost	280
A Moving Exposition	282
It Happened that . . .	283
A To-Do-List	284
Mirror of Reflection	285
A Literary Encounter	286
soberly, seriously	287
Shadows	288
Downfall	289
Believe It or Not	290
A Treasure	293
Dream-Ramblings	294
The Veil Lifted	295
The Poet's Seasonal Affective Disorder	296
The Letter and Its Aftermath	298
A Portion of . . .	302
Despite Improbability's Call	308
Treasured Memories	309
Wandering	322
The Timepiece	324
The Door	325

Table of Contents... *continued*

Inside the Aria	326
Adolescence	327
Child of Angst	328
Revision	337
Yearning	338
The Seasonal Call	339
Conscious	340
The Unspeakable	341
Anonymous	343
Valedictory Address	347
Off to College	349

Epilogue

About the Author	355
Other Books by the Author	357
What Others Are Saying	361
Editor's Notes	371
a few words from the Publisher	375

Acknowledgments

Raymond G. Allen, my love, only the two of us know what we have endured as I labored to give birth to *No Illusions. Through the Looking Glass*. It was difficult. Yet, it has all been worth it. Thank you for your amazing support. And, to my editor, hülya n. yılmaz and to Inner Child Press International, my sincere appreciation and thanks.

Preface

I had long thought of being a writer, especially, when as a child, my parents gave my siblings and me a desk for Christmas. And then, the following year, a typewriter. I envisioned sitting at the desk, putting my thoughts to paper, and then, stitching them into a book. However, at the tender age of ten or so, I could not type. My fingers were slower than my ability to regale my siblings with my tall tales, complete with detailed descriptions of the characters.

Somewhere, between those early years and a more recent major surgery, I let that dream slip away. However, while recovering, I signed up to take a writing class.

You might wonder how it was that I was able to write, in 2015, *Looking for Rainbows. Poetry, Prose and Art*; in 2017, *Dark Side of the Moon,* and in 2018, *No Illusions. Through the Looking Glass.* I sometimes wonder myself.

We all know that "tomorrow's intentions" may never be given a chance to breathe. Especially, when serious health issues intervene, which was the case for each of my three books. However, when one is doing that which one loves, as I was in writing, persistence, desire, discipline, and, with the much-appreciated support of my husband, who was working full-time, I overcame the obstacles that might have otherwise overwhelmed me.

Both in the cover art, "Mother and Child" as well as with *No Illusions. Through the Looking Glass*, I share with you my heart, and the gifts with which I have been blessed.

Jackie Davis Allen
Springfield, Virginia

Foreword

When it comes to the art of writing poetry with the idyllic leisure of a life well-spent, and having a tender, deeply-feeling heart, relating to the past and the present, you might be looking at the corner where Jackie Davis Allen writes her poems. The ingenuity of craft, brevity and aesthetic beauty she infuses in her work is unsurpassable. It has the beauty of sharp satire, delving deeper into the truth at times, telling a story she had either experienced or imagined to bring home a moral worth living for.

A mentor for the young, she leaves an indelible mark on the reader, whichever gender and age.

Her third book, although I am particularly fond of the first one, must be an improvisation of her poetic skill and mature thought. She keeps her word to herself and is selective in her readership, yet she plays with emotions and the intellect with the same detachment she herself exhibits while her protagonist, mostly feminine, is transformed into a precautious feminist, suffering and enduring all along while she is living.

Her nature has a touch of the American wilderness with its rich green and white snow, while she appears to be telling her stories with English tea beside her ficus tree, more than forty years old. You can narrate her poems among family and friends, and recite them in various gatherings. I wish her creativity to flourish even more and her generous pen to remain prolific. My high regards for her graciousness. I am proud to be her admirer and friend.

Sadiqullah Khan
Poet
November 4, 2018
Pakistan

Introduction

Jackie Davis Allen's third book, *No Illusions. Through the Looking Glass*, is a marvelous description of growing up in an impoverished area in the Cumberland mountains in Southwest Virginia. One can understand by reading this book how her first two books, *Looking for Rainbows, Poetry, Prose and Art*, and *Dark Side of the Moon*, took form.

Jackie and I grew up in somewhat similar circumstances in the 1950's, with both of us exposed to situations that could have easily been in the 1930's: She in the mountains, and I, on the far "down-east" coast of Maine, 40 miles from the Canadian border. Life was not easy in either place, but particularly hard in the coal mining areas of Southwest Virginia. We both learned tremendously from our extended families, and their trials and tribulations.

Jackie was a very bright, adventurous, and incorrigible child, that caused her much grief with her immediate family. She was often severely admonished for her apparent alien attitude. The fact that she can describe the difficult life she has led and the circumstances that shaped her development so well is a miracle, as her mere survival was in those times in question.

I know Jackie well, as we have spent the last fifty

years together. She was the first to be a college-graduate in her family, with much trepidation, whereas I was in a third generation of college-graduates, and expected to do well. Nevertheless, Jackie greatly impressed my family upon her first introduction. They knew immediately that she was something very special, and wondered about the luck I had in meeting her, when I was attending college in Virginia.

Indeed, Jackie is something special.

Her deep understanding and communication skills, as expressed in this book, bring one to laughter, pensive thought, and oftentimes, tears. We now know another truly gifted writer has been added to the family, and probably the best.

I urge you to read *No Illusions. Through the Looking Glass,* and experience the difficulties, joy, and sorrow Jackie has most perfectly expressed. When finished, you will have no illusions about the excellence of her writing, the content of her poetry and prose, and the descriptions of the life in those times in southwestern Virginia.

Raymond Gardner Allen
Springfield, Virginia

The Poetic
and
Prosaic Narrative

No Illusions . . . *through the looking glass*

Jackie Davis Allen

You Might Be Surprised

I wonder, who were you as a child?
Were you complacent, obedient, contented
Or were you adventurous like me,
Even a bit wild?

What were your thoughts, aspirations,
Your dreams? Did any of them crystalize,
Materialize, or did they exist
Only behind silent screams?

There are so many questions
I wish I had asked, probably just as many
Answers I have long forgotten. Life is difficult
When hiding behind a mask.

In the living out of one's days, I imagine you
With no map to follow, did the best
That you could. Perhaps, I have been walking
In a pair of your shoes?

Time cannot turn back the past,
And yet history often repeats itself.
I wish you could see me today.
You might be surprised.

Dreaming

I dream of climbing mountains,
Of flying over cliffs,
Of sailing high above the cloudless sky,

The world below me, a welcoming view.

How fortunate I would be
To find a place where love abides,
Where it permeates all walks of life,

Where man walks hand in hand with peace.

And where, beneath a canopy of patience,
Love scents the very air we breathe
With the perfumed fragrance of kindness,

Borne on the wings of forgiveness.

And in this dream, smiles as wide as the ocean
Are filled with the depth of understanding,
And man has come to recognize

The merits of compassion and grace.

In Those Days

In original handwritten records, kept by
The Daughters of the American Revolution
Some of my ancestors may be found.

On my mother's side, their travels from
Massachusetts to New York, then to Virginia,
Roots traced as far back as the 1600s,

They include names, relationships, dates.
Alas! The most revealing is the calling out of one,
A mother, who must have known better.

She, for uttering an oath, for striking
A neighbor; and, in black and white script,
It says she was removed from good standing.

After offering an apology and rendering penitence,
She was then returned to the fold. The record,
Remaining in the church's Book of Discipline.

Life Is a Tapestry

Life is a treasure, a biography
A tapestry, if you will, a party.
It comes with gifts, presents
Which you have received.
Perhaps hiding, deep down inside,
Waiting to be revealed.

So, come to the party!
Join in the weaving of the threads!
Both of your current and future life
Begin now to collect
The bits and pieces,
The brilliance, the gems
That reflect your uniqueness.

Seek out the kaleidoscope of light,
And with diligent determination,
You may design the fabric
For the person you hope to become,
The one for which you were born,
The one you were always meant to fulfill.

Me, as a Child

Never a quiet child,
In the matter of mischief, pugnacious
To a fight, I fought against the odds.
Though much of the time,
I was lying, confined in a cage,
Enclosed by bars, spread both narrow and high,
Escaping far beyond means, grief, worry or design.

A curious, adventurous child,
I spent my days and nights dreaming
Despite undiagnosed pain.
The pattern of my life was running
In circles, running aground, running out of gas,
Running out of time, so empty,
So painfully empty, except for the pain.

Needing a rescuer,
Mine came as a breath of fresh air.
A young physician desiring to lift me
Up and out from the white caps of fear, where
I languished in a sea of discontent.
Other healers, seemingly idle, stood
On the sidelines unconcerned, ill-equipped.

I moaned, prayed, dreamed,
Though not straight up and down.
And, as if response, with caring compassion,
And despite the scratching, shaking heads
Who said, "Her days are numbered",
I beat the odds, thanks be to God
And thanks to the physician whom I loved.

And, It Came to Pass

Herein, a compilation of mossy dreams, streams of thought, some wild adventures are sought. Revealed in prosody, in verse. A time mostly forgotten, or never known or chosen not to recall. It was a secluded place of silvered dreams, of uninformed young boys and girls, tarnished dark and old. With futures, bought and sold, indiscriminately, due to indulgent need and greed. Seams of anthracite and coal's waste befouled the bodies and the creeks with impunity. Indifferent, polluted as they were in Appalachia.

It was an ancient, settled place time forgot, where with strangling hands, coal wrapped itself around the thirsting throats of men coming back from the war. Like other men who had spent their lives, they slept in bed with the horror of nightmares tattooed on their minds.

Elders never talked about the olden days, when they or their ancestors were young, growing up, trying to make their way in the only way they knew how. Though, some of their children now had choices, at least for a time. Education was the tool with which they used to carve out a better life for themselves and their families. They hoped because they loved the mountains, even as fear draped its blanket over their dreams, obscuring vistas, both the real and imaginary. Unable to see past restraints, they dreamed dreams, too many of them impotent to bear fruit.

Days came as they would. One made of them the very best they could. The angst of weeds and toils grew faster than those of greenbacks or blades of grass. Yet, they placed their trust in the Almighty. Hope elevated itself as high as the tallest mountains, the rugged Cumberland's of Appalachia. A place, seemingly neglected. A place where the dialect paced itself along generations. Ancestors, six feet below, left only the legitimacy of their names. And some little acreage of their once huge holdings. Granted from military service. Their progeny, the seeds of which were like dandelions, prolific, so much so, that in the twenty-first century, the common surnames people wore, were those researchable back to ancestors who settled in the hollers in the 1700s. Little known, until genealogy's recent researching years.

For many, paying debts, getting ahead was the goal. The further one climbed, currency found there was best. With land selling for ten cents on the dollar. Sold to those who had attorneys. The sellers, understanding not. Except the few dollars in their hands. And, how to make a mark. Neither able to read or write. The evidence, a document.

Roads switched around the thighs of the mountains, back and forth, the curves like hair pins or switchbacks. A time came when the roads were paved. Paved until coal trucks carved deep potholes in them. Neither were any of the roads spared. Or, repaired. The potholes put to shame the ones Benjamin Franklin once wrote about. So much for society progressing, marching forward. Life was hard in the mountains where coal ruled as king. Creeks once ran clean and clear, run off from mountains. They played the part for fishing, for swimming, for fun. A blink in time's eye.

Some, befitting thieves, wore masks. Like sharks, they stole lives with reckless abandon. The diligent working class, longing, needing more of most everything. They survived, if they did, on bare essentials, prayer and hope. Plundering hands steered designs, crawled, snaked into virginal bodies of mines still in process. Confined neither to valley, roadsides, beside creek beds, at the foot of mountains, or perched on hillsides, north, south, east and west. The greedy needy trampled on the rights of those who tried to rise above poverty.

Huffing, puffing down, all around, some took liberty. Took what they wanted, more than they needed. The innocent, left behind, left as refuse, waste, in their trembling wake. Smoke, rock dust, plumes of discontent filled the air, all most aware, helpless to vent, to change their course.

The nation, unaware or uncaring.

Within the walls of the houses, some children of the female kind, old before their time, begat babies. At age fourteen, often younger. Of the fathers, the boys, the men, coal miners, one and all, they but victims, either fleeing or sitting on behinds. Blowing smoke circles, despairing hope. Or doing both, expecting, praying their polluted lungs be cleared from the coal dust that was certain to steal life. Just as it had for their fathers, brothers, uncles. The dreaded diagnosis was a death warrant, irrespective of age, years served. It came with sad finality that death was its sole claim to fame. And, proud, they guarded their names.

On the rocks of the masculine gender, in the graveyards that dotted the hills, carved on each, visible or invisible, were the words "Died of Black Lung."

Hollers and higher up roadsides dotted the landscape, blighted by expense of black gold. On rickety stilts stood many a house. Nearby, some log cabins, shacks, or shanty's, papered inside with newspaper.

Outsiders laughed when natives would not say "queer", natives saying "quare", instead. They who gawked did not realize they were foreigners, they who seldom visited, coming only when funerals issued dark and final invitation. What did they know? They were highfalutin relatives, nevertheless strangers.

None of us knew Shakespeare. Or that he said "quare".

Choked throats sported goiters for lack of iodine. Doctors, too expensive. Goiters popped out like apples, swallowed whole. For both, the old and young, diets consisted of collard greens, pinto beans, cornbread, anything that they could raise in the garden, or barter. The Good Lord giveth and He taketh away. Besides, we will be seeing Him, in the good old bye and bye. No need to ask or question why.

They were a God-fearing people. They prayed, backs bent on troubled knees, crawling on all fours, or else sliding on bellies into the coal mines. Coal marked its stamp on foreheads. Families were not spared. The cost was steep. It was deep and it followed everywhere. Even in sleep. The color of men's aging faces, blackened by coal, instinctively told the story that was swallowed whole, stuffed down in the belly of aches and pains that gained no fame. Anxiety grew furiously fast. Like weeds in a garden. Like yearly time of conception. As many as ten or twelve or more: sons, daughters. Bereft of excuse or persuasion of religion, children sired, born. Children needed to help out with chores. So much work to do.

Hand dug-wells offered up their bounty or not, the waters forthcoming or not, depending upon the rains, or drought. In times of plenty or want, families helping each other as best they could. Hands, calloused, labored, picking, scrubbing on the wash-board. Water, drawn cold. Bucketful by bucketful. Heated in galvanized tubs, outside, on rocks. Or on cinder-blocks. Tubs filled with water, propped up, a burning log beneath. Bubbling, blazing hot. Then, again, and again, trains. They spewed their waste, staining more than clothes.

Babes, carried on backs by mothers. Perhaps, another one growing in her tummy. A little laughter, a lot of laughter. Some from making love, making babies. Necks stretched out, too far, inevitable, a risk. The cost, great. But still, they loved and cared for each other, committed, loyal. Yet, purchase they did. From need, on credit, essentials, down at the country store. An *IOU* to pay, with the next paycheck. Not always possible. It rendered little fat after paying some on the bills. It left little to nothing to tide them over until the next payday.

Again, it happened. The words to a song became a people's own, sung with conviction, as in a hymn but needing a miracle instead. Sung with sadness: *I owe my soul to the company store.*

Children cried from nutrition's hunger. And from shame, with only a people's circumstances to blame. Such was the brunt of coal whose fires imprinted upon the many working themselves to the bone. That was the measure of a man. It was the same in houses of dread. Coal was king and all but a few bowed down to its call.

One's family name was said to be all that one truly owned. Guard the family's name, that was the suit of armor each family held in common. Or so it seemed. Guarded by children without the benefit of wisdom or maturity. Even still, they made the best of what they had. Guarding names without understanding, comprehending. Unless, it was the same thing that got so many to thinking. How was it that the elders seemed to know the actions of the young before they did the deed themselves? Parents worried, accepted gossip, rumors out of fear. The truth or not of the accusation, disregarded. Too often, believing the worst left children with no place to turn to for comfort. Perception of one's family name was guarded, worn with pride on backs of dignity. Carried in bellies, they slept with it at night. Even still, some lies, so easily said to a census taker, how he was blinded by deception, by pride.

Two wrongs do not make a right. A child breathed prayers for fear of a spanking for lying. And another, if caught out not having told the gospel truth. One for action of misdeed, and one for the deception. The unwritten rule.

As a banner, pride held high a flag that a mountain people needed. More than the want of radios, televisions, telephones, luxuries was the need to have a backbone. A strong need to stand up to strangers attempting to pry. Like that of the census taker, asking questions. None of his *daggone* business. What a joke!

A lesson taught, a lesson learned. Not the daily-practiced one, which with a switching found out each and every one of their children's sins. Like tiptoeing at night or during the morning, these rituals respected a father's need to sleep, despite ungodly hours. No way to conceal the noise, the sound of forgetting. Remembering too late.

Miners, fathers, coming home early or late, the need to sleep was real. The children went off to school in silence. Perhaps, there might be a change in shift that sent the fathers off to work at night. Coming or going, either way. Hard to know when, or if they would come home. Maybe, possibly, week-ends.

A picnic would highlight the mind.

Miners, slight, small, large or very tall, never was it a consideration, the miners unwavering in expectation. What they expected from children and their hard-working stay-at home-wives. Still, they did the best they could. Never mind impending death and always, taxes.

Life went on. Yet, on anticipated pay-days, a gift, a sacrifice of a dollar, or a candy bar. Changes have come. Some for the better. Others not. And still, in spite of it all, the people were and are God-fearing, hard working. And, then it came to pass when many left it all behind, seeking a different way of life. The roots to the people of the mountains, stained with coal, still call out in the night, begging for more of their stories to be told. Praying to be bold enough to overcome the taint of poverty's shame.

Determination

Desirous that I am,
Determined, staunchly so
To remain both loyal and bold.

I am offering up myself.

Sacrificing pride and ego
That my sensitive-self, stained
And sorely ripped asunder

From the ages of the past

Might offer lesson's hope
To those not so
Unlike myself.

Will you not come along with me?

Let us cultivate a garden,
One with new purpose.
A bed of roses,

In which we each may thrive,

Rising up to bloom in colors
That enhance each other's self-worth.
May our fragrance, our perfume

Find our days seeking peace.

Jackie Davis Allen

I Still Remember

"It's breakfast time. Wake up."

Something smelled terrible! It didn't smell like sausage and gravy, nor bacon or cooked apples with cinnamon sugar. It didn't smell like the biscuits had burned either. I wasn't interested in any breakfast that smelled like that. It was awful. Unlike anything I'd ever smelled before. I rubbed my eyes, trying to get the sleep bugs out, and said, "What's cooking, Momma?"

A skunk was the source of the foul odor. He'd been navigating around the building, and had released his scent upon being interrupted.

Momma would later repeat the story to my embarrassment. I'd cringe, as she and whomever she was telling the story to, laughed. Strange, the things one remembers.

I must have been about four years old at the time of the "skunk" incident. We were living in town, about a mile from where my grandparents lived. Town consisted of a gasoline pump standing before a stone grocery store, the old hospital building-turned-apartment building and a hotel. On the outskirts were houses, a theater, two churches and a small one room post-office.

Surrounding the town, the mountains wrapped their arms around everything. One had to look directly up into the sky to see the sun or moon, both appearing to be about the size of a skinny silver dime. Coal-mining was the number one occupation for men, although at one point, logging had vied for that position.

Few people owned their own homes, and other than in town, houses were separated by distances created by the curves in the roads. Mostly stick-built, the buildings rested either on stilts up against the mountain, in hollers, or beside the road or the creek. Wherever there was flat enough land to accommodate them.

One of Momma's sisters and her husband lived in the same building that we did. Auntie's apartment was in what used to be the Operating Room of the Old Hospital Building. One of their rooms had a floor that was slanted. A ball or even a marble, when placed on the floor, would roll across and strike the baseboard of the opposite wall. I early on decided that I'd best crawl to get over to the other side of the room, afraid that I'd lose control if I stood up.

To exit the Old Hospital-turned-apartment-building, other than by the front door, one had to climb down a steep incline, and there too, I was afraid. I thought I might roll down the hill, unless, I was on all fours. So, I crawled.

One morning, I woke up to find a teenaged uncle asleep in our apartment. He had a broken leg. For some reason, my Momma was taking care of him. I don't know why his own Momma, my grandmother, wasn't taking care of him.

Next door to the Old Hospital Building was the Old Hotel. I remember a kind lady. She was Miss Elgin. She had white hair. She either lived in the Old Hotel or else the Old Hospital, I can't rightly recall what she looked like. I do remember she was most kind. She gave me a Valentine one year, one to my sister too. Mine had Robin Hood on it. And, it was fancy. Robin had a feather in his hat.

As much as I liked my Valentine, I was jealous of my older sister's card. It had a princess on it and she was wearing a beautiful white ball-gown. It was sprinkled with diamond dust. And, the princess was wearing a diamond-studded tiara on top of her head, long blond hair flowing down her back. It was all just too marvelous.

For years, these two Valentines were tucked away for safe-keeping in Momma's cedar chest. Once a year or so, they were taken out so that we could handle them, and then, having dreamed and or imagined adventures, the cards were replaced in the cedar chest. Under lock and key. Until one day, Robin Hood disappeared.

Jackie Davis Allen

so old, the story

heavy with clouds,
the sky; beneath winged feet,
the scented air

a honey-suckled breeze

in spite of history, comfort, family
I sing songs, dream dreams
of something more

yet, kneeling with eyes downcast
and with head bowed
I beg pardon

relief from mournful cries

blue bruised, scoffed, unfairly scorned
great are my responsibilities;
demands of family ride hard my back

a lighthouse of hope,
I pray to find; pray, too
some divine revelation

to come near

Indian Summer

Beneath shivering trees, colors fall at my feet.
Above, the autumn sun is shining down its light,
And with the cooler days and nights, I think.
By summer's retreat, Mother Nature is sharing

Some of that which gives her delight.

A blue bird sits, rests, on the lonely fence.
The rails are split, worn, distressed in an ancient way.
The wind protests invitation of the season's sixth sense.
By Nature's prerogative, each has its own reason to stray.

Below the bare-boned trees, leaves sleep in defeat.
See how the autumn sun shines down a golden light,
Wearing nothing but a cool breeze and how,
In ways mostly indiscreet, Mother Nature desires

To share some of her color and her might?

Any, who over life are singing, hovering,
See the birds fleeing. Flying south.
Hear their songs of mirth. See the man?
He works, his heart beating, entreating.

Beneath the trees, leaves now blanket my feet.

Jackie Davis Allen

Moving Day

Tucked back into the Cumberland Mountains of Appalachia, where the Justus and Smith clans had lived since the mid-1700s, the only people who lived around us were those of Momma's people.

Poppa's people were from Tennessee. And since that was a far-away place, we did not visit them very often. Living in a tiny apartment, we never had overnight visitors, except, and unless you count, when my uncle broke his leg.

When Poppa came back from the war, we lived with his sister and her husband over in West Virginia. I had no idea that my mother was expecting a baby, but in September of the next year my big sister and I had another sister. The apartment we had moved to and were living in was becoming crowded. So, Poppa contracted some men to build us a house. Now that the house was ready, we were moving again. But it was raining, raining cats and dogs as people say when it is pouring.

In spite of the rain, we were off, Poppa driving the "rattle-trap" truck up the winding road that snaked between the mountains and the creek. Momma, my two sisters and I sat across from Poppa. We were like sardines squeezed into a can. I am thinking that Poppa must have borrowed the truck because it would be years before he would be able to purchase a vehicle on his coal miner's salary. Our belongings were packed in apple baskets and cardboard boxes and shoved onto the bed of the truck, or else propped up wherever there was space. The couch and mattresses had a tarp over them for protection.

I remember Momma saying something like, "Honey, I wish you had had the men build in a small room. We could've used it as a nursery, and later, when we could've afforded it, we might have put in a bathroom in that space." I suspected that Momma was expecting another baby. Maybe a boy this time? Poppa just looked at Momma, as if to say, I was barely able to make the last payment to the men.

No Illusions . . . *through the looking glass*

The road was littered with leaves, stuck to the hardtop by coal-dust. And the light rain, which continued to fall. Avoiding coal trucks hogging the other side of the narrow, barely-two lane-road, Poppa gripped the steering wheel. He moved close to the side of the road and avoided going off the side of the embankment into the creek. Not an easy thing to do in the rain and fog of a wet and windy morning.

Just a little further and we would be home. Our new house: four rooms, a front porch with wooden steps. Once we came around the bend of a hairpin curve, there'd be a barn, and a mountain stream. The stream was the dividing line between my grandparent's house and the barn.

Grandpa owned a lot of land. In fact, he had given Momma the land that our house sat on. He'd given her a choice between it and an adjacent flat piece, the one that I wanted. But Momma had her reasons as to why she had refused it. *It's too close to my Momma and Poppa.* I did not quite understand what she meant. Both pieces of land had space for a small house, but there, too, both sites backed up against the base of the hill, the mountain, where shale and slate crumbled and slid down. A little ditch ran alongside, separating our house from the road, about six feet away. Our house sat on stilts, about four feet up off the ground. Someone laid a plank across the ditch, turning it into a little footbridge.

Perhaps, it was Poppa who lifted me down and out of the truck. Maybe, it was one of the men whom he had hired to help us move. Momma would later say that she could not believe how much I remembered about that day. Once I crossed over the little footbridge, I stepped onto the wet soggy ground that made up our yard. My white anklets and sandals changed colors.

I climbed up the wooden steps to the porch where I sat down in the swing. It was suspended from a bead-board-ceiling, painted blue. The blue color was supposed to keep the flies and bees away. None of them were flying. I think they were hiding from the rain and the cold. I tried to stay out of the way as our belongings were carried into the house.

Jackie Davis Allen

It must have been late autumn.

Like the weather, I was wet and cold.

Looking Back

When I was a wee child,
Wild, and within a heartbeat
From the top of the mountain,
Freedom came uneasily.

Momma did her best
To keep me close, to keep me alive,
Safe from the coal trucks, those
Scary monsters on wheels
Huffing and puffing; ferociously
Empowered with adolescent
Fury, the masculine kind.

Alas! Serendipity and
Undiagnosed disease
Conspired to deprive me
Of vitality.

Whether by miracle or not,
I cannot say, but inspired
By creative need, its desire
And my need to play.
I denied eventual diagnosis,
Proved it wrong, to God
Be the glory.

It was the driving, thriving voice
Of the license propelling me
Toward the goal, the gift
Of claiming for myself
A new kind of normalcy.

Jackie Davis Allen

A Most Memorable Day

The town is filled with the pride of miners who've come to pay their bills. And, perhaps, as a treat, a trip to the five-and-dime for a bag of popcorn. A rare thing it is when they've some spare time on their hands. Or any money to spend when there's time.

Main Street is a narrow, two-lane-road, smack down between the mountains. At home, we have to look straight up into the sky to see the sun, the moon. Anything that flies. Same here. And, the sun, well, you'll find this difficult to believe, but it comes around to our house only around noon. Until then, the mountains hide its face.

My sisters and I are standing at the open counters. Ben Franklin, no never mind! I want one of those hair-bows. My mother doesn't seem to agree. To impress upon her my desire, I wait until I see she's otherwise occupied. Then, I snitch a blue one, not taking a chance to take more than just that one. Lest she catches me taking that which isn't mine.

Slap! My hand stings as Momma smacks it; back into the arrangement goes my ill-gotten gain. The pain of mine is not unlike hers, for I've pinched her thigh, twisting it, to let her know what I think. A whack on my bottom! Soon, we are creating a scene. But leave it to my mother not to care when she has a mind to let me know what's on hers.

Heads are a 'turning, my bottom is a 'burning, and far too loud, I confess, is my wailing, complaining that Mr. Smith wouldn't miss, from all of the huge display, the tiny little bit of thing I wanted. Momma was not happy. "Mr. Smith has to pay for everything you see here. Young lady, you've come close to turning into a thief."

Further attempts to dissuade, ensued. My sisters and I tried, unsuccessfully, to convince her to change her mind. Momma lost her patience. But, like a vigilant store detective, seen in a rare movie, Mr. Smith came strolling down the aisle. He had smile on this face. I almost missed it because I was hiding behind my mother's dress.

He told her to pick out something really nice and that he'd give it to us as a gift. Perhaps a tricycle, some night gowns, slippers? But no. We wanted what we wanted. And the scene which we created wasn't what anyone wanted. And, so, Mr. Smith offered up a solution.

"Take the children on down to the dress shop. Let them select whatever they want, and tell them to put it on my bill. Tell them that Mr. Smith sent you all there."

To the relief of all those shopping, we left. And, I imagine Mr. Smith was happy that we'd left his store. People could continue shopping without wondering about those unruly children, of which I was the loudest. Problem solved?

Not so fast. To my mother's dismay, and the dress-shop-keepers, too, we turned up our noses at the expensive silky party dresses. I remember they were turquoise. Something that would have spared Momma from sitting at the sewing machine for hours and hours.

We three wanted what we wanted, no never mind the cost. And, what we wanted were identical black, white and yellow striped cotton skirts. They had elastic band-waists. Topping off the skirts were white eyelet, embroidered halter tops, made of soft cotton. The tops had lace flouncing all the way around the front and the back. So pretty.

We were all tired. The dress shop was small. The aisles were close. The shop was one we had infrequently walked by. But never, ever had my mother the nerve or the money, to consider entering. The sales-staff, my sisters and I and Momma, all frustrated. None of us were in a good mood. Momma sighed, as temper tantrums, again, ensued.

So, as to escape the burden of her unruly children and their misbehavior, Momma complied. Out the door we misfits happily went, the shopping bags filled with our heart's intent.

Jackie Davis Allen

Heart-of-Gold

Matthew was an old man
Long before his time.
It was black diamond's coal dust
That stole his breath and deprived him
Of his days, long before his time.

Slight in stature,
Wiry strong, he labored.
For love of family, hearth and home.
It mattered not the hour.
He just labored on.

Of options, he had few
To none. Of responsibilities,
More than some.
Of aches and fears,
He shared them with no one.

So, when the trumpet sounds
And the day of reckoning comes,
I pray old man Matthew
And his soul might be rewarded
For his sacrificial heart-of-gold.

Bee-Balm Garden

Stoically standing,
My aromatic garden smiles
As she patiently awaits
The arrival of a vast number of guests.

Well-dressed hummingbirds,
Painted butterflies, wearing colors
Blue black, orange, yellow
Striped, spotted; jewel toned.

Stunningly beautiful in nature
And, of course, I would be remiss
If I did not mention the robust
Buzzing bumblebees.

Honeyed sweet is the nectar
Of my bee-balm's showy flowers.
Strikingly red in color, plentiful,
They succor the thirst of the hummingbirds

For greed, for satisfaction, for delight,
For more than mankind's discerning eye.
My Bee-Balm Garden offers up her bounty
In exchange for spring's demise.

Jackie Davis Allen

All the Way

My father worked, sacrificing his youth.
Back bent, night and day, weary.
A coal miner, wiry, strong; determined,
Desperate with breath compromised,

Persisting, yet, to the bitter end.

The size of compensation, slight.
For his wife and children's needs,
Little commensurate. Despite anxiety,
Depression, they wondering at what point

Coal would run out and he might lose his job.

He never complained, though often
In pain, injured or recovering; a wrist,
Slit from an errant slip of an axe,
He returning to work no matter, that

Waiting-to be-chopped off, a finger-tip.

Always present, the hacking cough.
Breath lost, the price paid for daily bread.
Few knew, other than coal-mining families
How suddenly, irreversibly Black Lung

Destroyed the quality of a man's life.

Time

Time, memory, a race
Living in the past
The present

Walking, running

Toward the future
Climbing
The ladder

One racing ahead
At breakneck speed
The other

Struggling

Panting
Trying
To keep up

# of a moment left wanting

of a moment
left wanting
like moment
in time

that comes
as thief
in the dark
there waits one

with intention
of resolve
ready, willing
to pay any cost

like moment
in time
that comes
in drunkenness

of wakeful nights
intentions fade
on resolve's
wings of flight

shamefaced is he
who counts not
the moment
of loss

Fancy the Concept

Crumbling shale, slate, in color,
Like pastels in a box,
They slide down, landing on the ground.
And, I am wondering how they came
To project out from the hill
There, where no grass or blossoms grow.
A puzzling mystery that invokes creativity
As I select a first one and then another and
Discover that they serve as chalk
For marks I make upon other rocks.
Nearby, see the dirt, the soil upturned
To make the site upon which our house
With sticks, was built? A little pot
Was uncovered; one made by the hands
Of an ancient child, one, who with clay, made
The tiny object, its lid, upon which I saw
But for a second, both crumbling like dry silk,
The dust and only the memory remaining,
Like the words, the ones I wanted to utter,
The ones I withheld, the ones that waited
Until the adults were finished
Which, by that time, I had forgotten
Whatever it was that I might have wanted to say,
So, I suppose I saved them up for a special day
Where now they find themselves
Overflowing into poems or pieces of prose.
The past, filtering through a screen
And of the present, I see more clearly
The film in slow motion, morphing
Into who it is that I have become,
No regrets, tears or second-guessing,
My life has become, as unto a book.

Jackie Davis Allen

Moment of Brilliance

What night is this, which is so velvety
That even the mountains, the moon, the stars
For a time appear obscured
That my voice becomes

An aria of echoes
A message to the heavens
And to all the constellations
As I lift up myself in praise of mystery?

My heart leaps
A passionate rhythm, keeping time
With the early dawn's expectation,
Like the vision of a shooting star.

It seems a quickening streak,
Burning as it passes
Through the earth's atmosphere
Then, brushing the mountain tops

With its golden dust, a meteorite falls
to its death. To where? God only knows.
Extinguished.
Except for its treasured memory.

While the Candles Burn

Some candles burn late at night. Hot wax
Drips as the sun rises. And as from need, one
Man works hard, neither indolent nor lax
In his duty. A book lies on the table.

A holy guide, faithfully he follows
Its tenets. Labors he in the work-field,
Breaks bread with others, shares his wine.

Yet, there comes a thief, who waits beside
Envy's road, one who neither labors nor loves any
Other except himself, thinks he only to steal
Their labor's effort, their gold

Their livelihood. An easy way-out, he shuffles
Cards of cunning's deck, ridicules work-ethic.
Shall fate then place a noose of guilt

Around his neck while candles continue to burn
Late into the night? While heavy sweat still
Drips down from a laboring brow? Shall tears
Reign down mercy and remorse on predator's face?

He, who in shrouds of sloth, deceives by pity's cry
Stakes claim that to which he has no right.
Conscious denied, he who toils not strives neither

By morals or hard work. Therefore, shall thirst
Of avarice ever find satisfaction? Shall he who
Drinks from jealousy's cup pay the price, or
Shall he repent, having discovered the light?

Poesy

With the years
Convening, above and beneath
The covers,
Woven from the threads of mutuality,
Creativity has surfaced
As a frequent form
Of communication.

Yet, of emotional
Distance, dare I say,
Its face often
Finds itself
Inserted between
Verses, stanzas.
Perhaps that is the reason
Why tidal waves
Crash with poetic rage.

Who Am I?

I am me.
I am more than you can see,
More than you can perceive.

Inside this shell,
I have lived the life
Of both poverty and plenty.
Enough to have walked
In the shoes of many,
And though I know few
Of their names,
They and their situations
Bring me to tears.
They, my brothers, sisters.
And, I as a daughter, sister,
Wife, mother, teacher
And a child of God,
I give thanks.

Blessed be the Almighty!
And, if it be his will
And I am allowed more
Of his bounty,
The question is:
Will I continue to use
My creativity,
My inborn abilities
To morph into still yet
Another identity?
One other than that
Already associated
With my name?

Winter's Might

The other day, I spied a spider.
It was on the window sill,
Frozen in its tracks.

I looked at it. Its eyes stared back.
A web of silk it had spun.
My silk blouse and it glittered

In the winter's sun.
On the ground, snow's white
Uttered not a sound

About what either of us
Had left undone. And then,
I began to think about the future

Of what it was I had yet to do
And what of time remained for me.
Suddenly, five fleet-footed deer appeared.

In a second, they disappeared. And,
Winter's blanket of might erased
The evidence of what I had seen.

Midnight Prayers

O Lord, I am so weary. It's dark and cold
I'm heavy with child. I'm but twenty-and-five.
My children are in number four, ranging
From two to just above six. And, how
I am to manage, I don't know.

There's little coal for the stove.

O Lord, I am tired and out of work.
My wife is in labor and I'm praying
The doctor soon will arrive.
With each of her groans, I ache.
Even as I pace the floor, I am thankful.

My wife's sister has come to help.

O Lord, I am worried about my sister.
The snow is heavy and the children, awake,
Roused from sleep, at the table they sit
Bewildered, why at midnight are they not
In their beds. I pray as I wait for the doctor.

The roads are treacherous.

O Lord, I am the doctor, and I have come
Up the road to deliver a baby. I think the mother
May be having twins. They're coming early.
I'm afraid for the mother. The hospital, far away.
The odds are not good; I pray all will go well.

What I fear most is the unknown.

Jackie Davis Allen

Revisiting the Scene

The bitter cold that descended
Down from the mountains
In the late of night
      Was more white and bold
            Than that in my little snow globe
                  One that left me shivering

And the mournful moans
Of the swirling winds that sifted
Down and around
      Mimicked the name
           Of the troubled town
              Where we lived

The cozy four-room house
Once as quiet as a mouse
Suddenly was disturbed
      By an ungodly scream
           Like one I imagined coming
              From a feral cat

The scream, such as it was
Was unlike any other, yet
It competed with my little understanding
      For in the bed, in the next room
           My Momma lay in agony
              The bed posts securely bound

By pristine strips, torn
From white sheets
Spelling for a time the searing heat
      Of pain, words for which
           I am at a loss to explain, then did
              The fog of fear finds me shaking

No Illusions . . . *through the looking glass*

And rendering my mind
Into the form of a jigsaw puzzle
That made no sense, nor did
    The ungodly hour that found me
        Listening to the blood curdling wails
            My Momma pleading for relief

My Poppa and my auntie
Paced the floor, grim-faced
Praying not to lose control
    As they waited, as Momma waited
        And as I waited, I wondered
            Whatever could be the matter

A whisper, a word uttered
Laboring, was she laboring
Like my Poppa who worked
    Down in the mines? But no
        She was reminded, it was not time
            For her to push, not yet. Wait

The house, otherwise, was hushed
All of us waiting for my Momma
To smile again, waiting
    For pain and fear to go away
        Waiting for the doctor
            Praying he would come right away

And, then a knock at the door
A face identified as the doctor
In the window-pane, welcomed
    But not his muddy tracks
        On the floor, nor the remains of a cigar
            He was chewing, chomping on

Behind the trembling curtains
In a shade of bluest turquoise brocade
Substituting for a door, he went, devoid

Jackie Davis Allen

Of his offense. He, carrying his bag,
    Would he help my Momma
        Make her well?

And, then, with grunting
And groaning, and words
Encouraging her to breathe
    My Momma let out a shriek
        And followed by slapping sounds
            I heard wild kitten-like cries

And there she lay, delivered
At last, from the worst of the pain
For a moment at least, in either arm
    She, holding the twins, a boy and a girl
        And Poppa and auntie, exhausted
            Ushered the doctor out the front door

You must understand
That what I share comes from
The well of a child's memory
    Grown old with the years
        And tears where holes
            Probably still exist

It is what I actually remember
But as the days passed
And pneumonia invaded
    Their little lungs, each one
        Passed away, only a few weeks separating
            Each little twin's demise

The frozen ground stayed around
All winter, and yet, my Poppa
Wrestling with his and Momma's grief
    Went down to the basement
        Where he fashioned a wooden box
            To send them back to God

No Illusions . . . *through the looking glass*

I watched as he labored
The sawdust, the boards
Taking shape, and I wondered
    How to make sense of it all
        The silent little pale faces
            It was beyond understanding

And soon as the first thaw
Poppa and the men-folk
Drove up the road, and up
    On the hill, at the mountainside
        Cemetery, they dug the tiny graves
            With mattocks and shovels

The ground gave way
And so, they placed them
In the ground, dressed
    In dimity dresses that Grandma made
        One for a boy and the other for the girl
            I still hear Momma wailing, despite
                The train in the background

Jackie Davis Allen

Her Royal Inadequacy

Shout and scream without ceasing,
That is what she did,
And as the thunder
And lightening chimed in,
I cowered in my seat.

Shame and embarrass without impunity,
That is what she did.
The day darkened with anger, rage
And I, shaking, was so afraid.
No outlet for an escape.

Ruled by fear, humiliation,
A dark closet awaiting
Over my head, a key dangling.
She, laughing derisively, and
I, wheezing, at a loss to understand.

Tape on my mouth for talking,
For being; heed the warning.
Keep it on, do not take it off!
The room spinning around.
Am I dying? Why is she smiling?

Years later, upon the street, she.
I see, her proud eyes I dare not meet.
Forgiven yes; forgotten no, nor the reign
Of terror that shook its tyrannical fist
At me, and my inner child.

Window of Expectation

The question that kept growing deep inside
At the age of six or more, was
Who were Dick and Jane.
Oh, I knew they were characters
In my pre-primer reader, the ones
With perfect everything, doing perfect things.
Yet, I had never met anyone like them.

Dick and Jane rode bikes, flew kites
And skated down sidewalks.
Something not possible for me.
There were no sidewalks
In the mountains where I lived.
No cash, nor place to buy bikes, skates or kites.
Was it possible there were children like them?

Everything was perfect
Between the pages of Dick and Jane:
Fathers wearing suits and carrying briefcases
And mothers, with hair all curled, wearing heels,
A dog named Spot, running all around
With children like Dick and Jane, saying
Run Spot, or *See Spot Run.*
Who ever lived, or talked like that?

Years passed, far past the age of six,
With perfection imprinted on my mind,
Impossible, yet a tantalizing dream goal.
So, I wandered far in my imagination
More than the seventeen miles to town,
Waiting for the day, waiting for the time
When I would be out on my own.

Jackie Davis Allen

Sitting on the Fence

Like some decision sitting on a fence,
The day is cold, chilly, changing colors;
Alternately, snapping to attention,
It poses at the photographer's bidding.

On the porch are two empty rocking chairs.
They, moving idly back and forth as if
Recording a mournful song of the day
That a dream, a desire faded away.

Like adolescents, some teenagers are
Predictably unpredictable; of life's moods.
Some hot, some cold, some
Often unable to choose wisely.

Yet, there stands one, who, seemingly with
A magic wand, persistently studies, works
To create life with a developing gift.
Still, another asks, "What is in store for me?"

Searching for the Magic

From a seed, an idea began to grow.
All that I needed was a cardboard box
To hold all that I owned
And, I would be ready, ready to go.

At the appropriate moment,
I would be off on an adventure.
To where? It mattered not.
Me and my cardboard box.

Utilitarian, conserved, practical, rare,
Most appreciated, none to spare,
I persuaded my grandmother.
Received it from her, thankfully, as a gift.

I prayed, stayed within the parameters
Of being good, as best as I could;
Prayed serendipity should arrive
With a light, to make for me a pathway.

Prepared, willing, I would be whisked off.
Me and my cardboard box, away
From boredom into a magical world, where,
On wings, I would soar higher than ever before.

Jackie Davis Allen

Dinner on the Ground

Fried green tomatoes
Wilted lettuce salad
Corn bread, pinto beans
Some collard greens

Green beans, corn on the cob
Sliced tomatoes, coleslaw, cucumbers
Pickled beets, chicken and dumplings.
It's time for Dinner on the Ground.

Fried-apple pies, stack cake
Blackberry cobbler, banana pudding
Chocolate pies, homemade candy.
Can't wait until the preaching's done!

High on the hill, the graveyard
It's Memorial Day, where sermons
Are preached for all those passed away
Back in the winter. We'll be here all day.

Come and eat! The men rush forward,
Most already on their feet. They're the first
To be served, to eat. Then, the children,
The women get what's left over.

Hymn's sung, prayers said. Eulogies read.
It's the same as it was back in the olden days.
Perched high up on the hill, next to God,
There's nothing like Dinner on the Ground.

Observation

Scampering up the trees,
Climbing further and further out,
Venturing out beyond, long tails

Balancing from behind.

They swish back and forth,
Leaping from limb to limb,
Seeking the best place for a nest.

They offer a seasonal respite

As in preparation for relief
From the world's worrisome wars
And its partisan predicaments.

Should not both man and beast play, work?

And exerting effort and energy,
Might not they keep up with responsibilities?
Yet, I do fear some shall never survive

The season of their resentment, their discontent.

Jackie Davis Allen

Confessional

Inside dwells the real me
As in a not so-cozy bed-of-rest.
I was, I confess, a wild child,
Meditating upon the largest
Of ideas. The creativity,
Waiting inside to come out
Into the sunshine of life

From a tender bud to an unsuspecting,
Unfurled, a blossoming flower.
I sought out, as best I could,
Within captivity, a way, a path
To freedom, the means
By which I could set free
My impending identity.

My thoughts christened me
As a wild child,
Endowed with imagination,
Yet one without the wherewithal
To please or satisfy
The longing residing
Deep down, inside of me.

On bended knee, while climbing trees
I prayed: "please God,
There must be something more
Beyond the mountainous walls.
Something that will enable me to climb
Over the obstacles, that prevent me
From being the one you want me to be."

No Illusions . . . through the looking glass

The Child

No one was within hearing distance.
If they were, they ignored her crying.
And so, she learned a way around her pain.

Closing her eyes, she hid inside and there,
Playing games, plotted how best
To circumvent the infliction on her body.

She hid beneath the bed, behind the door.
Her room without a lock. So, using her mind
At the appointed time, like clockwork.

When the instruments of medication
And their willing and able inflictors
Wheeled the cart down the hall

She flew outdoors, bare-feet, winged,
With nightgown flapping, no wind or breeze
Required, just the impetus of churning wheels.

Outdoors, free as a bird, taking refuge.
Not in a tree, but behind, blowing
Bubbles, unaware of clues surfacing.

Sweet the occasion to exercise, to make use
Of her legs and mind. Too long, lying idle,
Lying in pain. I confess. I was that child.

Jackie Davis Allen

My Mother's Mother

Ancient and most old, in middle-age.
Time's evidence piling up.
White braids on top of her head.

A look of consternation, mine, my
Grammy in bed. She, consoling me,
Uncovering the awful scar,
All the while smiling through the pain.
She, explaining the necessity.

Something far beyond
My tender years, startlingly brave,
Telling me what the doctor said.

And I aghast, afraid of the meat-cleaver,
Sliced-clean-skin, flat
Unlike the other; it, a plump
Melon, once a twin,
Now an orphan. All by itself.

I'll be fine. It's just a matter of time.
And what I said to my Grammy,
I don't recall. Probably, something like,

I was afraid you'd die, and she,
Smiling, wiped my eyes, replied:
"I'm more than o.k. Please, sweetie,
Don't cry. I'm all better now.
I'm not going away."

Forever

There is no future
Without a past
And in this moment
With your arms
Around me
May the present time
Forever last

Fearfully Formed

The house was cold and quiet,
Except for the creaking floorboards.
My breath I held in check.
Lest it betray my presence.

My eyes, focused
To my shock and surprise
On what lay upon the frosty white.
It gave me such a fright.

Before the window-glass,
Fearful, yet determined, I stood
Trembling. To steady myself
I placed my hands, apprehensively

On either side
Of the window-frame.
I will not deny that I shrieked
So forcefully that my voice,

My fear, breathed out a fresh coat
Of ice, upon the window-glass.
Or, that it erased the evidence
Of that which had so terrified me.

Garden of Grace

At play in the fields of the mind, I stumble over the weeds of the ever-present-past, weep copiously over the dark clouds now descending

On my head, torrentially raining down like hailstones, from which I fathom there is no escape. Despite many attempts, I am unable to hide.

At work in the garden of grace, I seek to find my place, and from need, I kneel down upon the verdant face of the sweet earth.

And giving effusive thanks that the sunshine of forgiveness has granted my heart its peace, I find my heart filled with meaningful purpose.

Jackie Davis Allen

The Thief

An inveterate thief
A spender of time
Procrastination steals, both
From the rich and the poor

Thinks only, he
Of tomorrow, the next day
Maybe next week
Sometime next month

Perhaps in a year or so
Motivation will rise up
With inspiration and he will begin
To wipe away his fears

Woe, pitiful is the man
Who spins such a spiel,
And persisting, encourages misery
To become his closest friend!

Delirious

I climbed out of the window
Into the boiling cauldron
Of what was a sizzling summer day.

Not a submissive child,
I carried with me my creativity
In all of its disguises, wherever I went.

Careful to remove the window screen,
One foot on the bedrail, I hoisted myself
Up and out onto the ledge, with the other.

I fled into freedom's playground.
Clawing at nature's roots, exposed
As they were, climbing up the hill

Steep with weeds, trees, brambles,
With bruising urgency, though they, not seen
As obstacles, nor difficult to overcome.

My mind focused on swinging, hurtling
Up and over the treetops, clinging to vines
Like Tarzan, until the vine in my hands broke.

Down, down into the darkness I tumbled
To a place where the sun found not its face
Nor its mirrored essence. So, I waited.

Yelled, listened, waited, needing assistance.
None forthcoming, I struggled
As in a fairy tale of the making.

Dawn

The golden blush
Of the early morning
Has found me once again.

Her welcomed face, a more
Brilliant a sun has never arrived
Upon the stage. See her smile?

Dawn has unloosened her robe,
Blushed as it came undone,
Shared with me her passion.

My heart raced, and as I drew closer,
I lowered my eyes, shading them.
Dare I look? She climbed higher.

Hiding in Plain Sight

Poppa says, "Don't cry, it'll make your Momma sad."

"But why, Poppa? However can that be? I heard her sobbing all night long, that's why I couldn't sleep."

"It's a dark and horrible thing that's happened; the baby, the one that passed away. He's in the bedroom in a box. That's why your Momma weeps and cannot eat or sleep."

"But why, Poppa?"

He turned his head away and sighed, and I wondered if he was remembering the cries of the baby last night, the one who now lies silent, still.

"Hush child! I hear someone. Our neighbors have come to pay their respects. It's a tradition around these parts. They'll grieve with us these next three days and nights."

Morning is cold, the pine board-floor creaks as I pull on my clothes, my feed-sack nightgown on the floor, in a heap; its color blurred and tear-stained design, I barely can see. "Come on in," Poppa says, as I stand around the corner, taking a peek at both the strange and familiar faces. "Make yourselves at home. Do come on in."
    Poppa's face is ashen, strained as he forces a welcome. And in the bedroom hovering over the baby, we all hear Momma weeping, wailing, praying, as she paces the floor.

"How is she doing?"

The whispers congregate back and forth with condolences, their sympathy showing in the furrows and creases that line their faces.

"Come, child, come sit on my lap."

An elderly matron picks me up and pulls me tight to her breast. Her ample bosom heaves and I feel sick at the scent of her perfume. It's *Evening in Paris*, in that blue bottle.

"Let the child go."

A kind voice notices my discomfort. And finally, I am released to return to my hiding place. Alone I am, with no one to share my pain.

The kitchen table groans beneath the offerings of our neighbors. Sitting, standing, they hold a plate in one hand and eat with the other. Have they forgotten my mother? The clock on the wall above the radio table ticks. I know its hands have moved from this morning because it's now lunch time, afternoon. The sun has buried its face.

A thick blanket of snow has covered the earth, the fire in the pot-bellied stove hums, and the dearly-beloved gathered, begin to sing, a lined-out chant of hymns. A shadow hangs low over our house even as the living room is aglow with faces, with hands raised up praising the Almighty, accepting that which cannot be changed. And Poppa, I see he's holding Momma in his arms. They're lying on the bed, near where the baby is, in its christening gown. Dare I go in and interrupt them? What am I to do? I tiptoe into the kitchen and find something good to eat.

There's chicken and dumplings, my favorite. Coleslaw, corn bread, pinto beans, and a little left-over apple butter stack-cake. I think I'll have some banana pudding, too. Sitting beneath the table, I watch the many pairs of legs moving back and forth, and back again. I wonder if, when they've had their fill, will they then go home? And, what of me, my Momma and my Poppa? Will we ever be the same? Will we ever sing songs and laugh and play again? Will things ever be the same?

No Illusions . . . *through the looking glass*

What is it, I wonder, that makes mourners laugh and smile when only moments before they cried and wailed as if the baby in the next room had been their very own?

In the darkness, I make my way into my room, climb into bed and pull down the quilts that Momma made. With my head on my little pillow, I snuggle with my rag doll.

I'll be alright.

I'll tell Momma and Poppa, if ever they ask, I'm old enough to tuck myself into bed.

I'll be good. No one needs to worry about me.

Jackie Davis Allen

Heart-Strings

Within my heart,
There is a yearning,
A song overflowing
With love and tenderness
For the least of these.

Within our land,
Our laws are being broken.
Violated, the little ones used
As pawns to tweak heart-strings
To make excuses, allowances.

In the air, disturbed, I hear
Waves of animosity,
Wagging tongues, waving
Flags of resistance, sheep
And disingenuous politicians.

Think what you will, but
While holding your child close,
Ask yourself this question:
Does a nation of law-breakers
Make you feel safe?

The Color of Fear

Time after time
Day after day
Week after week

Month after month
Year after year
Secrets are hidden

Yet everyone is aware
Of the unspoken
And of the one

Who fears
Being revealed, she tries still
To keep on singing

Jackie Davis Allen

Grace

A wooden bench sat on the sidewalk.
Its slats, spaced two or three inches apart,
Carefully observed, corroborated
By its back pushed up against the brick wall
Down below, lying asleep.

A young man fully clothed, yet not against
The weather, his faded thread-bare jeans
Revealed long legs, which in another life
May have belonged to an athlete; he, on a team
Acclaimed as a role model.
Yet, today, with thundering clouds
Threatening, the gathering crowds
Have nothing to say, perhaps wondering
Though, if he had passed away. But no.
He was most aware of averting eyes.

Intent, focused on the double doors,
Concerned more about the waiting feast
ahead. In expectation of menu's celebration.
They buried their heads, ignored him.
But then, a disabled man

And his caretaker appeared, and pausing
for a moment beside the bench,
One opened his heart, and with assistance,
His wallet, saying, as he placed a five dollar-bill
By the man's head, "But for the grace of God."

After the Rainfall

Morning has become as dusk.
It is a most confusing spectacle,
Dawn refusing to open her eyes.

The hour is focused upon her.

From morning's grayed face,
The earth sits and waits
Beneath milky, palest-white.

Silent are the shades of wettest green.

A glimmer of hope suddenly lifts.
And a shimmering light, slowly descends,
In step, with the golden orb's tiptoeing dance.

See now, how the earth smiles?

Jackie Davis Allen

On the Path Again

So sweet the journey!
The words used to arrive
Easily, without effort
For him, or so it appeared.

And, as if designed,
Coming from heaven,
Coming into fruition,
Shaped as intended.
So great the blessing!

A period of loss, a lull
In the season that nourished
His gift, flowers drooped
Faded, wilting, near death.

Day became as darkest night.
Then, appearing in a vision.
In the briefest of moments,
Insight awakened, alert
And wily, much like a fox.

Despite self-taunting,
Both he and his alter-ego
Refusing to accept defeat,
Chose, instead, to fight.

Today, I see him as a steward,
Receiving, laboring on the path,
Searching, finding his niche; and
Of his discoveries, he shares
So that others might believe.

Diary of My Discontent

The ironing board . . .
It stands at the foot of my bed.
The box on top waits to accept her last remains.
Somberly silent is the iron.
I am pressed down, hard and cold.

Alas, my little one has flown away!

Lord, have mercy on me!
My breasts beg to be suckled.
The warm milk flows a painful, useless fluid.
Heavy my heart. I am unable to assuage my grief.
The ironing board is a ghost. It haunts me.

Too weak to fight any longer,

I wash down with alcohol, my precious baby.
Clean and holy; new, innocent. And no more.
I dress her in dimity, a dainty night-gown,
Made with, grieving, loving hands.
My darling daughter, my precious child . . .

Lord, have mercy!

Embroidered flowers, pale pink, yellow.
Green leaves with silken threads, the gown
My mother sprinkled with love.
Pushing the needle in, out, up and down
Until she was satisfied.

Lord, have mercy!
Snow-covered, the cemetery,
Rime-frost like sentries.
An eerie scene, naked trees,
Standing silent like ghostly guards.

Jackie Davis Allen

And at their feet snow melts.
My tears fall as I weep

Upon the funeral flowers.
Pink, blue, yellow carnations.
The scent makes me weak;
So, too, the pleading voices.
Most persuasive, family, friends.

Lord, have mercy!

I hear them, caring not.
They beg, plead, cajole.
Nothing can they do
To dissuade me from taking
One last look at her face.

First Place

I am amazed, in awe. Just look!
His garden is beautiful; it is lushly blooming

Seeds he planted are boldly, profusely blooming.
And even the buds, pregnant, are not far behind

And, as if in a rush, each competes, it seems,
With the others as they race toward the finish line.

Jackie Davis Allen

Seeds

I met him as I was traveling
Down a dusty, unpaved road,
Little understanding, why the sky was blue.

And yet, he and I pulled some weeds
And sowed some seeds of hope.
I think it was because our hearts told us to.

Though the bemused man
Was a stranger and though neither
Of us knew it at the time.

The seeds we planted would indeed grow
From buds into promises. Generously,
Empathetically, they have since spread.

Amongst, between our families,
Friends, neighbors and foes.
Their fragrance, ah, so sweet!

A perfume that still scents
Our days, our dreams, our ways.
We have become the dearest of friends.

We are reminded that hope
Is the promise-seed that allows man
To make a difference.

So, should we not, one and all
Plant seeds of love, forgiveness
Mercy, blessings, wherever we go?

Summer-Rose

When last the rosebud bloomed,
Winter's cold upon their hearts did fall.
Considered they the reasons vast,
Impatiently, waiting future's call.

Ever so sweet, the blossom dissipated.
So too, the petals, withered, old.
Think now upon the one in flight.
Her loss more grieved than purest gold.

When last the rosebud bloomed, night
And day stood in reverence, awe.
She, attired in the arctic chill of frigid frost.
They, longing for her sweet cry, for her call.

Seeking to knit together a piece of prose
With bits and pieces of winter's might,
The words came out very strong and bold.
Nothing could they do, to set things right.

A dream they carved upon a window-pane.
A castle-like fairy tale, it brutally unconcerned.
And as the season of long-suffering lingered on,
They thought only of the baby, named Rose Marie.

Jackie Davis Allen

My Favorite Spot

My writing corner is warmly welcoming.
It is where I go, when I want to be alone.

It is where I draw from the deep well, the gifts
I have been given for writing poetry;
For the tales, I share with friends,
Some based in fact. Some not.

My writing table is an antique.
I found it at a yard sale, in a little town.

It bears the evidence of a rodent
Having aggressively gnawed on one leg.
The table is a survivor, gathered up, refinished
By another who loves stories behind his finds.

My chair is Queen Anne, a vintage armchair,
Belonging, once to my father-in-law.

He and my mother-in-law lived
In an antique house, circa early 1800s,
Still standing in a town called Columbia Falls.
Not far from the Canadian border.

Winter's Solace

The snow flutters slowly and softly.
A blanket of purest white. What a delight!
Such striking beauty, no two flakes alike.

But heavy is my heart of longing
For the one who lies so low
In the cold and hardened ground.

My tears mingle with melting,
Silvered shards of splintering glass.
Heavy is my heart of grief.

Longing I am, for a final embrace
And another glimpse of you.
Instead, I am sitting by my window.

Your photo gazes down from the mantle
And I, weary, climb down the steep stairs
Of the night, searching for release.

The wind continues to howl
While I, stooping low, reluctantly,
Lower a wreath of flowers.

I place them on the cold stone
Beneath which your head rests
And leave with you in my heart.

Jackie Davis Allen

A Picturesque Scene

With the advent of spring, peeping
Up through the grass, fresh and green
Tiny heads, they are the tops of dandelion
Flowers. When organically grown,
Their young green leaves,
Cooked and served, are so sweet
To the taste. But oh, those yellow flowers,
They are such profligate pests,
Unsuitable for eating.
And when overgrown, their puffy heads
Become a child's play, seeds blown,
Carelessly scattered, needlessly
Shamefully, seeded into the lawn.
So, as for me and mine,
I do so prefer the solid mass
Of meticulously trimmed green grass,
Fescue, that is bordered by shrubs and trees,
Red maples, dogwoods, and lilacs.
The latter that breathlessly kiss
The watercolor-blue-painted sky
That wave their arms
Royally high, with banners,
Announcing with joy, the delight
Of celebrating an original painting
Of nature, and, if you will,
The creative efforts
Of my gardening acumen, which, when
Enhanced by nature's issuance of time,
It all stands as a sublime expression
Of springtime's sun-dappled residence.

Lack of Communication

The disaster's drumming disturbance
Damaged his reputation.
It eroded confidence in any predictability

Of the weather's forecast.
For yesterday's stormy weather,
A disaster, had been miscast.

Once the rain was over, streets reopened
And the clouds had beat a hasty retreat.
I quickly mailed a complaint.

Addressed it to the one at the station,
Expecting a prompt response
And some quick action.

Eventually, my letter came back,
Without redress, stamped
Moved: No forwarding address.

Now, can you tell me why I should not
Have been surprised, that the weather
Was not as had been advertised?

This Morning

This morning, I awakened
To skies gray and wet, and as
From the high heavens above,
Streamed down, torrents of intent.

From my window seat, I spied
A small squirrel, dark and dank.
He was shivering, chattering.
Then suddenly, he wisely scattered.

A bolt of destructive bright light,
Startling burst into fury's flames,
The clouds, revealing copious tears,
Released their pain, their angst.

No matter the name of the season.
No matter the time of day, or of night.
Nature delights in revealing different
And surprising aspects of her face.

Once hidden from view, I now
Welcome anew, the face of the sun
Bestowing ardent kisses
Passionately, bravely bright against blue.

Crossing high over the morning sky,
I receive a gift. A needed reminder.
It is a rainbow, God's promise.
His covenant, graciously renewed.

Garden-Song

My garden is a treasure. It contains
Such dappled shades of beauty,
Dainty blossoms rising above the green.

A stray lavender one entices me
With purple and yellow throat, it leans
Against the gray, board-and-batten fence

Nearby, in an isolated patch of sunshine.
Yet, within kissing cousin distance,
Another flower, rose-white, snuggles up.

The baby of the family stands newly tall,
Received as a gift, a friendship tree; hopefully,
It will flourish and bloom again next year

And reveal its namesake as a redbud tree.
How it enhances the fringes of the garden scene!
See its purple flowers and charcoal-black bark?

A bevy of perennial black-eyed lasses
Meet my own blue-green; we realize
That our time remaining is limited.

Let us dance and sing frivolity's song!
For life is a gift to treasure. Like my garden,
It is a gift to embrace. To enjoy.

Jackie Davis Allen

Of a Time Past

The tinkling of a bell
Announces twin horns. One chipped,
Sure footed, mooing, Betsy meanders,
Searching for pasture. Above, the engineer
Toots his horn, brakes screech.
They spark, metal against metal,
Now coming to a stop, soulful eyes
With tail and hips sashaying,
She moseys on beyond the railroad tracks.
Never the wiser.
The sun, hot; the wind, a chill.
A din of five men escaping
For a moment besides, beneath the rise
Of the railroad tracks. Intent. Intense.
They sit on hardened haunches.
A deck of playing cards,
Matchsticks. Their currency. The Devil's handiwork
Interrupted, they look up. Stern,
Accusing, abusing, a young woman
Stands. Hands on hips, harsher words on lips,
She chants a tiresome song,
Interceding on behalf of each lad's
Belabored other half,
Play like boys. You do
Play with toys, do you not?
The house, the baby, the garden
Tempt you not to care
To comfort or to rock
To sleep away some of the cares
That drag me down so deep.
I fear my shoulders are too burdened,
My heart, too weary, this life, to keep.
Chastised. Convicted, the din scatters.
Coal-dust, drifting down. Scattering
In the wake, beneath their feet,

No Illusions . . . *through the looking glass*

The kings, queens, the jacks,
All their patronage.
She begins to wail, to weep.
The swoosh of the engine, backing up.
She wipes her cries. Soot-stained apron.
No surprise. She straightens, stands,
Sighs at the sight, approaching the creek.
Tiny stick-figures, husbands, lovers
Laid off-idlers, scattering,
Hurrying now across the footbridge
To the winding, snaking road.
Waiting at home, the devil.
To pay, or worse,
With anger spent, she lifts up
Her suffering soul, climbs down the hill,
Crosses over the creek and trudges
Up the road toward home.
The mountains stand, silent witnesses
To her prayerful plea
For pardon, for relief. She,
Lifting up to God her wounded self.
Crying, "Would, that I could find such joy,
Playing like those boys."

Jackie Davis Allen

Time's Benevolent Grace

The face of the sun failed to greet the morn',
Even as the hands of the clock crawled
From time's uncertain path to the crest of the mid-day.

The mountains, as they were want to do,
Played hide and seek games with the golden orb.
Held hostage too long, the sun's face finally showed.

And I, no longer a child,
Wept for the loss of my youthful
Ways and days.

Revisiting the hills where treetops kiss the sky,
I looked back on my innocence and smiled
Despite more than a half century having its way.

The angst of memory's coal-pain left its imprint
Cold and as dark as the Norfolk and Western
That puffed clouds of smoke, staining everything.

Long into the recesses of the night, the dark ghost
Rumbled down the railroad tracks.

Whether real or imagined, I lay there in my bed
Where rusty springs and barbed fingers hurled darts.
Conscious of my need, I begged forgiveness.

In need of grace and out of fear that I would arise
And find myself reopening doors to actions, sins
Of commission, of omission, I begged mercy.

The Umbrella

I cannot say
From what perspective
She decided to go away.

From where I stand,
All I can say is that I am bereft.
I have lost a good friend.

The days, months, years
Promised to stretch long
Before us, a sunny demeanor.

The umbrella beneath which
We walked hand in hand
Until the great misunderstanding.

With eyes averted,
She chose not to meet mine
No matter how much I tried.

Someone Is Watching

Woven hath he
Such a wicked web,

The melancholy bed
In which he lies.

Slowly, surely,
He is being chased

By words and images
That refuse to die.

Mistreated

Abused by a so-called friend,
By word, not deed nor actions,
Once she was a merry soul, laughter
Lit up her eyes, her voice danced with glee.

Yet, mistreated she was, by her lover
In conversation, by attitude. She was
Cursed, despised, alone, lonely, sad.
She prayed, God have mercy.

So, you ask, why is she weeping? Why
Does she remain simply his victim,
Attacked now, both in word and deed?
Dear God, how much longer?

Is this her fate? What did she do? Why
Is he against her? She used to be
The epitome of kindness, gentleness.
Her generosity, her love knew no limits.

But it seems he is blind, cares not that
She wants only to be understood,
She wants to live life devoid of conflict,
Devoid of strife, devoid of evil.

The stress has rendered her a skeletal-like
Paper-doll of the shining star she once was.
Now, with her brilliance drained,
She is but a fragile essence of herself.

Jackie Davis Allen

Good Day

For most of us, the day begins
With simple things
Like waking up, feet planted
On the floor, one before the other.

We greet the morning, sleepy eyed,
Too often annoyed.
The alarm clock, insisting,
We respond to its command.

Realizing that this day
Going back to sleep is not an option,
A man or women must arise.
At least until it is time to retire.

Or, so they say. The lottery tickets
In the jar are but a reminder
The last time we promised ourselves
It makes no sense to ever buy another.

And, yet we do, we did. They are reminders
More than a slap in the face. So, with purpose,
We turn to greet the morning,
Jump in the shower, and in the privacy

Of its cleansing waters, the scales,
The dead pieces slide
Down the drain, and unthinkingly,
We fall back into the same old routine.

We have repeated it over and over, millions
Of times. Accuracy here, unimportant.
Except, perhaps, to accountants who insist
We report that we began to work,

No Illusions . . . *through the looking glass*

At the age of seventeen, not sixteen.
So, we wrap ourselves in a thick towel,
And briskly, against the coming hour, attempt
To massage away any disagreeable thoughts

Of driving off to work, or catching the bus
In the dark, only to return in the dark.
The daylight, seldom seen. Except
In dreams or otherwise on weekends.

Responsibilities, bills, family, health
A paycheck, the inducement to keep
Up the standard of living, fear
Of falling behind, thankful we have jobs.

Education is the ticket with which we climb
The steps on the ladder to becoming.
Still, we walk out the door, trusting in God,
Ever mindful of those who are suffering.

The Golden Ones

Now that the drizzle
And the fog
Have finally fled the scene,
The golden girls gaily frolic
Amongst the mossy green.

Like ingenues on a stage,
Hoping to be selected,
To be invited to participate
As guests of honor
At my annual tea party.

Ah! So many.
Each named Susan, black-eyed.
They attired in frilly skirts,
Painted in identical shades of gold.
See, how they embrace the space?

Enticed by the admiration
Of passers-by, they flaunt
Their beauty as if posing
For a magazine's
Upcoming photo-shoot.

No Illusions . . . through the looking glass

On the Right Path

How many summers had she awakened
To sweet kisses of lilac's scent, to birds,
Each singing their part, as if on stage.

Her cap's tassel, she moved from right
To left. Bedecked in white, she marched
Down the aisle. Arm in arm with her dream.

The tickets thus purchased, she rode high
On waves. Nearby, the news. Ten months
In the making, he breathes a silent lullaby.

As if on stage, life continues its routine.
A dog barks. And, inviting a collection
Of imitators, they create a noisy scene.

So too, the wind's brisk breath, it causes lace
Curtains to do a little dance. Causes the bones
Of the window to make of morning's gold, art.

The floorboards groan. Here and there,
Between the hands of a ticking clock, soft
Crying. It reminds her of her own thirst.

How many mornings had she awakened
To the cock-a-doodle-do of Old Red Top,
He exercising his inherited rights as a rooster.

Wrapping up her interlude, she, with a smile,
Returns to her books, her studies, dreaming
Of that which has yet to come.

Jackie Davis Allen

At My Desk

Within poetry resides mysterious voices
Of the past, the present, sometimes the future.
My muse whispers their secrets, private thoughts.
She urges me to take dictation,
To record their messages,
Which, I, the poet, faithfully do.

With a blank journal, I consider my pen.
My computer, staring enviously at me.
And as I wait for a Voice to come,
Soothing strains of classical music
Fill in the empty spaces of creativity.
Will my Muse awaken one of the Voices?

I ignore invitation of heart palpitations
If a Voice doesn't quickly materialize.
Breathing deeply, I continue to wait,
And am surprised that my Muse has sent
An unfamiliar Voice, one unrecognized.
Nevertheless, I begin the poetic journey.

As I take dictation, I am barely aware
Of what it is I am writing. A bounty of words,
A few more and suddenly the page is filled.
And the Voice, silent, mute, is no longer there.
I wonder at the significance of what I see.
Could it be that an alien actually guided my pen?

Old Red Top

Head cocked, with red comb glistening
In the morning sun, he heard the enemy.
Saw that they were coming after him.
Stumbling, trembling, attempting to flee,
Old Red Top turned around only to see
An army advancing, in number three.
No alternative did he have, nothing left to do.
Except to attack the enemy
Fueled by anger, by revenge. Filled
With rage, he lifted his wings. The fight,
A battle, began, his honor to defend.
Surely, his intent was to silence the giants,
The child-like giants, the ones with foaming mouths,
The rabid ones who towered over him,
Hurling slurs. And he, wild and crazed, resolved
To diminish their incessant badgering.
All the while, the Lilliputian giants taunted,
"Old Red Top-Old Red Top-Old Red Top".
And the play became a frenzied battleground
When Red Top swooped upon his target.
He tangled her curls into a bloody mess.
A pre-adolescent child, devoid of innocence,
Her skulking cohorts retreating, fled
While, she, fighting for her life, begged mercy.
Atop his struggling prey he crowed, victorious,
Proud of conquest, triumphant, mouth dripping wet.
But then, a weapon raised, aimed, fired.
Despite the smoke, it was apparent Old Red Top
Was no more for this life. And while ignorance, guilt
And remorse found their shame, the three
Agreed, never again to play the taunting game
That put Old Red Top in the stewpot.

Jackie Davis Allen

The Snows of Tomorrow

Wearily wandering through the mountains,
I came upon a stream of water
Flowing from the rugged hillside.

Cool and frightful was the breeze,
Upon which offensive visions of the past,
Like thunder before a storm, painted the sky.

Vines twined themselves about
Ancient and twisted trunks of time,
Wrapped themselves around heart's

Sleeves with scant secrets, serving up
Hints of tarnished treasures, drab-gold
And some ruins of faded rust, dark and old.

Arms alarmed. Nearly all stripped bare,
Forrest freely revealed its damped carpet
Of switchback sorrows lying beneath

Strong and fearfully-built dark feet.
Moistened by tears and fears, day lay.
Discolored, dying, unrepentant.

Summer's death ghostly mocked
The incandescence diminished. Yet, despite
Autumn scenes, worrisome clouds screamed.

No Illusions . . . through the looking glass

A Summer-Morning

I hear Grandpa's footsteps,
Then sense his hand on the doorknob
While the creaking hinges sing their familiar
Early summer, awakening song.

The door opens
And then it snaps shut. Not quite awake,
My face burns. His beard feels like
So many crawling red ants.

Aroused, awakened, annoyed,
I brush him away only to find
Myself engulfed with an invitation
To gather up my hoe

And to follow him
Up into the fields; fields are what he calls
His many garden plots, his orchard,
High up in the mountains.

Off, as to battle, we trudge.
The trees, the forest are a jungle
That awaits errant thoughts emerging
Of the enemy awaiting. The hot sun, blazing down.

An aching back, the weeds resisting,
I am determined to do my part,
Supported in part by Grandpa's defense:
"She's just a child!"

Furloughed for a spell,
I trek down the steep hill, avoiding the rocks
Where snakes and varmints reside;
Where, at the cool mountain spring, I arrive.

Jackie Davis Allen

Water gushing, refreshing my thirst,
My attitude. Back up the hill, I go,
Rejuvenated, perhaps to do what I can
To help my aging grandparents.

With thoughts of strawberries
As a reward, I hoe up-side down
And down-side up, as if to break
The boredom of laboring in the sun.

I make a game of it. "Not so",
Says my weary Grandma; with a pail,
Instructed not to eat too many, the rewards
Provide an easy relief for both of us.

sibling rivalry

siblings are we
but oh, so separate by virtue of personality
admiration reserved by one's mirror reflected
as jealously insidiously inserted itself
    rendering the other something less

                    leave me alone, let me be
                        a loving sibling to you
            not the one to be ordered around
                    diminished by your stature
                as you shine in the limelight

we siblings, competing to be the best
each striving to be number one
all the time you ignoring my requests
insuring that memories would reveal
    what now can be shared

                    leave me alone, let me be
        what God intended when he created me
                      the person I felt I was
                  evolved in spite of the fact
            you thought you were always right

siblings, aging are we
yet still so separate by virtue of personality
admiration grudgingly given by one
effusively by the other
    rendering the one less, and the other more

                you left me alone, I became me
            the me that God created me to be
          sensitive and kind, gentle and loving
       thoughtful, and generous and considerate
       all reasons for me to be proud of me

• • •

Jackie Davis Allen

I Am My Mother's Daughter

Momma dreamed of muddy waters.
They visited her from time to time, with creeks
Swollen to overflowing, filled with sweat,
Blood and tears, and years and years of fears.

In each retelling of this story, cold chills climb
Up and down my spine, the hairs on my arms
Stand at attention, amidst the goose bumps,
Remembering the time, Momma tried to explain

What the muddy waters meant. And, I playing
The fool, denied any such belief or truth.
How could any dream, bear such terrible news?
I asked if she truly believed a dream could foretell

The future, or that which had already happened,
Wondering why she felt compelled to act.
Undeterred, my mother explained in simple terms
That even I, then a child, still remember today.

The muddy waters mean something terrible
Has happened, or is about to. Out of necessity,
I must find out what it is that I can do.
In my memory, I see my mother.

She's packing up bits of food, canned milk
A blanket or two, following her own rule, of which
She has parroted to me, more times than I can count:
"Where's there's a will, there's a way.

And, I am willing to find a way; yes, child!
I dreamed of the muddy waters again.
I best be going off to see where I am needed.
Something awful has happened or is about to.

No Illusions . . . *through the looking glass*

Maybe, someone has died during the night.
Or, there's a sick baby or some hungry children.
And I've been chosen to receive the message.
I'm off to do what I need to do.

You don't know how often I've answered
The muddy water's call, gone, come back
Before you children, ever woke up.
Someday, you'll understand, my child."

I have to heed the call, the message
That God has seen fit to send my way
For me to be an instrument of his care.
The Lord works in strange and mysterious ways.

When I have the muddy water's dream
I must, of necessity, go. Even if all I have
To give are condolences and my love
So often they just need someone to care

And to grieve with them, thankful too. For often
I'll find them with no food in the house.
And though suspicious, I, my mother's daughter,
Something similar has been passed down to me.

It has caused me to backslide down the ladder
Of negating superstition. I, the one who used
To seek out black cats to walk in front of and ladders
Beneath which to walk, found myself in direst fear.

Slipping back into my grandmother's wise counsel
Of not repeating a dream before breakfast, she
Who used to say, "Don't be telling your dreams
Before breakfast or else they'll be coming true."

Jackie Davis Allen

So, what was I to do with the fearful dream
That prevented me from getting out of bed?
Against tradition and my better judgment
And ignoring my trepidations, fears,

I shared the dream so difficult to relate
About the awful fate of the sailors.
I had seen in my dream, all drowned,
Providing such horrible specifics that we

Were chilled, down to our bare feet,
We listened to the radio, comforting us not.
It confirmed the young sailors of my dream
Had, indeed, drowned, in full dress uniform.

I can still see them in my mind's eye,
Wondering why they were standing at attention.
Did not they know the canoe would tip over,
Stirring up the waters, the muddy waters below?

I question why I was unable to call out.
Perhaps, I was afraid they would see me
Through cracks in the shack, showering.
Why was I showering anyway? In a shack?

I have no answers. Except, perhaps the dream
Proves that I am, indeed, my mother's daughter.

A Taste of Orange

Oranges of the past, difficult to come by.
Back in the mountains, when I was a child,
Available, at enormous expense.
Otherwise, packed in brown paper-sacks
For Christmas, along with candy and nuts.

Eagerly awaited, appreciated, thankful.
Let me be honest: I once associated oranges
With medicine, like cod liver oil
Taken against will, taken on schedule
For whatever ails; expected to remove.

The bitterness of the after-taste.
Eagerly awaited, appreciated. The one
Comprehending not where they grew, difficult
To understand. The weather, agreeable
Always in picture books, the sun shining.

Why did the sun hide its face,
Always arriving late at my home?
The oranges, arriving in excess
In the south, unlike the orange
Beneath. My chin was not the only focus.

And he, in his fumbling, his body too close,
Drew ever nearer to mine, chin to chin.
The orange and I, disinterested participants.
The orange passing back and forth, meandering
His face, his body, disturbingly too close to mine.

Jackie Davis Allen

The Midnight-Hour

Off to town, at ten cents a head, the theatre
Was my babysitter. With Momma and Poppa
Shopping bargains, markdowns, filling hopes
Of cheer for their wanting children, including me

With dreams that were simply that.

It was a time, when in the traditional mode,
Christmas was celebrated at my house
In ways that mostly mimicked the amount
Of money left over or not, from paying utility bills

Or paying some extra off, to the company store.

To bed, to sleep, to wait, to greet the hour
Of midnight, when gifts piled up beneath
The dining table, for want of a Christmas tree.
No TV, no newspaper, to make me any the wiser

For what it was that I might have requested.

To wake up, or to pretend to, after a time in bed,
The midnight-hour stroked, really the alarm clock,
And to run to the dining room. Waiting, a surprise
Of oyster soup, tamales, or something just as exotic,

An adventure before the opening of gifts.

A mask of pleasure met, in measure the tempo.
The hidden disappointment, no need to stress
Or sadden my parents about the wrapping paper.

No Illusions . . . *through the looking glass*

Newspaper comics, the Sunday ones, in color.
The cord and twine, saved up all year long.

In number three, the gifts I received, always.
In total three from my parents. The effort
Of creativity, imagination, ingenuity, and frugality
Hard to obtain, an orange, something homemade

And an extravagance, like a fancy handkerchief.

I remember with fondness the anticipation
Of Christmas, of going to church, of singing
Christmas carols, of the bag of candy the pastor
Handed out as I left the sanctuary, and the fun

Visiting my mother's parents at midnight.

Hot chocolate, cookies, chocolate-covered cherries,
Stories told about days gone by, Grandma and
Grandpa singing, snuggling, thinking
Of gifts all laid aside for the greatest gift of all:

The celebration of the birth of a special child.

Jackie Davis Allen

A Fine Shade of Pink

I sorted through my party dresses, just two,
And decided upon which one to wear.
I chose the soft pink eyelet-embroidered one,
The color of which was pastel lipstick-pink.
A dress a princess would be proud to possess.
Perhaps, this time, it would bring me luck
And ease the pain that bruises my memory.
For you see, my Momma made it for me
To wear in a May Day performance at school.
The dance was cancelled, sadly.
And so, with shiny black patents on my feet, a smile
Beaming from the inside of my green eyes,
I twirled before the mirror, giddily pleased
At what I saw looking back at me.
And off to my cousin's house I skipped.
Crossing over the bridge, I was careful not
To step on any cracks, her birthday gift
Safe in a brown paper sack. I gaily danced
Up the steps and entered the party room
Where gathered both boys and girls.
We, sitting in a circle on the floor; my skirt,
Spread regally around me then scrunched
As a green bottle sat waiting in the center
For a game, one I was unprepared to play.
No way to escape. So, I played.
And when the green bottle stopped
Spinning, its greedy mouth seeking
And finding me out, I blushed.
With eyes downcast, I yielded
As the boy planted a kiss, my first,
On my lips. All because I had no way
No other way to pay the fine.

The Mystery Behind the Doors

Fears rumbled like mounting hunger.
The morning sun oozed, tar melted the path.
On a dare, I entered the sanctum.
The church beside the road.

There, a glorious fever was in full swing.
Trembling, I sat down on an aged-worn plank.
Walnut, seat stained, the bottom lot where
Stood the whitewashed building, anon

Where nearest to the door, with eyes agog,
I swatted flies, and wondered if I should depart.
Mesmerized, I saw people shouting,
Saw foot stomping, the laying on of hands,

Dancers shaking tambourines, they, unlike holy
Rollers, receiving the gift. Speaking in tongues
I wondered if interpretation might soon calm
The frenzy. Or, my lack of understanding.

I waited. To no avail. Then, wondering if
Handling of snakes would commence
With forked tongues, tainted with evil poison.
If so, where were they?

I almost fainted. The pitch-level increased.
I prayed in silence. God, of the Universe,
Grant their wish, but may I not be identified
As either a believing or disbelieving guest.

Jackie Davis Allen

A Daughter of Appalachia

The 1950s were a time when bare feet and Kool-Aid were the highlights of the summer. It was a time when the circus never came to town except in dreams, and when hunger existed more than in my belly. And I, wanting something more, though not knowing what that might be.

The ticking of the wind-up, key-wound clock kept time with my slow, lazy days. Energy expended, exhausted from swatting flies who escaped the yellow sticky fly-tape hanging from the ceilings. There was no other movement. Except for the constant up and down the road of the monstrous coal trucks. Or, from the porch-swing gently moving to and fro beneath me. I stared up at the blue bead board ceiling from which the fly-tapes hung.

On the back porch, canning jars waited for my reluctant hands. Waiting in tin tub of soapy-water. Waiting for their swishing and swashing. Work in preparation for my helping Momma with canning the day's garden produce. Shiny glass jars lined up, sparkled in the sunlight. I'd soon be sweltering over the stove, watching the pressure cooker do its sputtering job.

Babies crying, suckling, crawling. And I, ever watchful over the little ones who joined the family every other year. Little ones increased the leaves on the family tree, though, I, unaware of the genealogical phrase, nor any names beyond our grandparents who might have resided there.

Night-dreams made of finest stardust shone over all, yet traveling, either by day or night, most actively was traversed in my imagination. We were isolated by financial constraints and anchored by coal mines, ruled over by all-knowing and all-powerful coal kings. No magazines or television to make us any the wiser.

Peasants, the coalminers and their families, children too, all bowed down by the heavy-weight and toil of coal and dust. Consequences of class structure and lack of education, increased anxiety and black lung shortened lives. The private lives of those non-union families whose credit might be withheld, at the one and only company store.

Embarrassment and loss of pride surfaced when "Charge it" was the only alternative to going hungry. The interest grew as did our hunger for something more. Urgency increased for high marks in the hope of escaping off to college. There to find something more, something outside of the confines of coal-mining and disability. Knowing broken hearts would result once their off-spring moved away.

Pressures mounted. Lives were shortened by rock-dust, lack of insurance, and limited transportation. Or from mounting pride which refused to seek help until life-and-death-circumstances forced one into action. Heaven forbid, if one's house caught fire, especially, during the winter! Or if one's father became unable to work. Or lost his job in the mines. Seems it always happened to someone we knew. Still the name, the family name, held in high-esteem and respected at all cost, even to the point of lying, taught one a lesson. To be poor was to be avoided.

Vacation was something the rich indulged in. Children of the coal-mining class shuddered when September rolled around, as in the dreaded assignment, "Write about what you did during your summer vacation". Didn't teachers know that "vacation" was only a word? A word in the dictionary. A word to coalminers' children found in the dictionary most of them didn't own, found only at school.

Light bread, we called the white-and-sliced kind, the one that became a mayonnaise sandwich. Often, there was little to no meat. Light bread became so treasured that I, sometimes, went to bed with a saved slice under my pillow. The envy of all, come morning. Light-as-a feather-biscuits. Yum! Made fresh each morning by my mother, made with lard rendered from Grandpa's hog. Lard was supposed to clog up our arteries. I heaped these heavenly biscuits with blackberry jam, the berries of which we had picked alongside the railroad tracks and back into the brambles. We purchased wild blackberries at fifty cents a water-bucketful. My mother bought all she could afford. That is, until some wise one, in charge of the railroad tracks, sprayed pesticides over all, and in so doing, decreased our meager food supplies.

Chunks of roasted pork, oh how wonderful! Salted as well. Delectable morsels shared by my grandparents, until it ran out. The only meat except for a chicken when company came. Never enough to go around, lying to convince others that the back was the tastiest part. Parting with a chicken, a huge sacrifice, as eggs would be no more. Company, more important than my mother having enough to eat herself. She decried that anything more than the wing or back was as tasty. I cried inside, knowing better.

Lye-soap, made on hog killing-day, a mysterious rite. My parents kept me away, lest the lessons be too difficult to comprehend. The killing, the blood, the smoke, the fire, the lye, all left to the adults. Something not for children. The "how" it was done, to me, still unknown to this day as is the apple butter-making. The butchering, the fires, the kettle. All too dangerous for us children to be around.

Lessons taught and learned by a mother who knew best. And backed up with the surety of knowing her children, at home, under her watchful eye, were safe from harm. We all lived, tented and closeted from the rest of the world between the twin mountains of want and need. Hope reigned eternal in the breasts of those mothers and fathers whose whispers and shouts and dreams depended upon, "Where's there's a will, there's a way."

Eventually, Momma's will for me came true. Fortunate was I to win several scholarships, merited from desire's effort, grades and economic situation. Not without my mother and father's watchful and guiding eyes overseeing my work. My life flew out of the mountains of Appalachia and soared on education's wings. Since then, time has taken me to places that neither my parents or my dreams could have ever imagined.

Whimsy

Patience was not, nor will ever be,
One of the cards I had been dealt with
In the growing up seasons of life.

Neither was compliance to rules,
Written or unwritten.
Unless, they made sense to me.

In my limited experience,
Rules seemed to arrive
Upon the scene, as if by chance.

"Willy, nilly", making no sense
To the impetuous, incorrigible.
That was my alter ego's name.

The repertoire of situations,
Boundless, into which I thrust myself
I found insufficiently satisfying.

Nor did the ways and means
Momma sought to confine me
Within four walls, under her control.

The game I liked best to play, I created
On my own; and depending upon my whims,
The rules did too. Whenever and if ever I so chose.

Jackie Davis Allen

Peace, an Elusive Truce

It has been a long time
Since we saw one another.
I cannot remember
The last time we spoke.

Life's intrusions have exacted a steep price.

The distance between us
Is like a rugged mountain.
The silence is an obstacle.
It booby-traps intentions.

In surrender, I am waving a white flag.

Inspiration is sorely needed.
Motivation, too, to break
Through erected barriers
The old issues we cling to.

I miss you, am sad you choose not to respond.

Why can we not choose
To take on the armor
Of grace and forgiveness?
Can we not find a truce

That allows us to go forward?

Between Friends, Neighbors

There is a structure, a fence,
Down below my garden.
It is in need of repair.

With intent, I have attempted
To do it all by myself.
Sadly, I have met with no success.

A new plan, I have come up with.
Indeed, I think it might work
If I am met halfway in the design.

And, with my neighbor's consent,
We agree to build a bridge over
Our differences; perhaps, even add a gate.

What merit is there in resurrecting
Old grievances, some having roots
More than several generations old?

Might not the breach between us
Remain in the past, if we use the tools
Of mutual respect and forgiveness?

Jackie Davis Allen

The Idiom of the Day

Watch that smart tongue, little miss!
Watch what you say!
Or else, I'll have to wash your mouth
Out with a bar of soap.

Don't you be following
In you know who's shoes! It'll
Get you into a deep well of trouble.
You'll not get away with it.

For sure, it's in the Good Book
Where we find our sins will be found out.
And certainly, I'm not saying
That I'll be spared that scrutiny.

Little miss, or should I say
Much more strongly, young lady?
You ought to know better by now:
A lie is a lie. It smells not of the truth.

The Purloined Papers

Sally and I scurried down the road. We lived just four houses out from each other. Neither of us could see the other's house because of the mountainous terrain and the way our houses were situated. Our destination was a church, an ancient stone building, about a mile from where the two of us lived. The pastor and his assistant were bachelors and frequent guests in my home. Because we had no phones, they would often just stop by. We seldom ever knew when.

We breathed a sigh of relief when we discovered, as I had anticipated, the door to the church was unlocked. The cool and darkened sanctuary greeted us, but what we were seeking was downstairs. We were intent on just one thing. We had planned it out very carefully. I was supposed to be out at Sally's house and Sally was supposed to be at my house. Neither of our mothers knew that we were not at either place. What were we thinking?

I showed Sally where the outdated Sunday School materials were. We took only the ones that were dated several years past, leaving the current ones undisturbed. We reasoned, or perhaps, it was I who reasoned, that the teachers would certainly have discarded the outdated materials if they had but taken the time to go through them. Besides, if I were to have my own school, I needed them and I would certainly use them. Before we left with our treasure, I had another idea. "Sally, we need a hymnbook." And Sally said, "O.K. Let's take one."

What transpired next was an exhausting effort to coordinate the careful removal of, first, one page from one hymn book, and then, the next page from the next hymn book. Over and over, from one hymn book and from one church pew to the other. We often had to stop and double-check what we were doing. I had no idea it would be so difficult to keep track of the pages I was tearing out and the pages Sally was in charge of. So as not to duplicate our effort. It seemed as if it took hours and hours for us to complete our task.

Finally, we had everything we had come for. And more. What an exciting day it would be when my younger siblings and my cousins met and I could teach them. They would not have to wait until Sunday. And, they would not have to wait until school started in September.

As Sally and I walked back up the road, we found it difficult to conceal the papers we had lifted. Fortunately, no one stopped and offered us a ride. Questions about what we were carrying might have proved difficult to answer. We soon came upon another church building. Its rooftop-mounted loudspeaker was silent. On Sundays, however, it broadcast the Gospel to all within hearing distance. Sometimes, in unknown tongues. We sat down on the doorstop to rest in the small amount of shade that it afforded. The Norfolk and Western coal-cars chugged along behind the coal-fired steam-powered train on the hillside. Just above the creek, and higher still, the mountains rose. "Sally, do you want to help teach?"

"No, it's your idea, but I'll help you if you want. Why don't we send out invitations?"

"Good idea. I have a little pad of paper that we can use. I think we should invite the little ones. If we invite our big sisters they'll just try to take over."

"You're right; we'd better get going."

The sun had finally come around to the side of the mountain where our parents lived which meant it was almost noon. Although there was a slight breeze, it was hot. I was tempted to try my teeth on a tree's umbrella-shaped leaves to use as an umbrella. But I did not. Those leaves were difficult to separate from the tree branches. It sure would have been great to have had a parasol like Mamie's. I had seen her walk past my house many a time, wearing all white and carrying a white parasol, that's what my mother said the fancy type of fabric umbrella was called.

Mamie was related to my family in some way. But I did not know how. I thought she was a bit strange. And, I was somewhat afraid of her. She had had four or five husbands. She ordered them from a catalogue! I wondered what kind of catalogue that was and wherever did one find a catalogue like that. I wondered, too, what she did with the extra husbands when she decided to order a new one.

Sally and I continued to walk up the road, occasionally shifting our burdens from our arms to holding the papers on top of our head, so as to shield our heads from the sun. A mile can be a long distance when one is in a hurry, like we were, needing to get home so we could hide the papers.

"Let's see. We'll invite Sissy, Sal, Petey, Katy Bird, Peg and Milly. Anyone else you want to invite?"

"No. How come you all have those funny nick names?"

"Grandpa gave them to us. Are you going to invite your brother?"

"No, he's a pest."

I did not say anything but I agreed. He was about a year older than I. He didn't play fair and that was not nice.

Once we got past Sally's house and came to mine, we decided to hide the Sunday School materials in the basement where the ceiling was a little less than five feet high. The floor was compacted dirt. Somewhere along the line, Poppa had decided to underpin the house with cinderblocks. He had some men help him jack up the house to its current height. I could never understand why he had not raised the house up high enough so that he could walk without stooping over. The basement was where Momma and Poppa kept our garden produce. Downstairs, where it was dark and cool.

It would be several years before Poppa had some men help him dig out the rest of the basement where he would have a coal-fired furnace and an electric well-pump installed. All the canned goods, the waiting canning jars and the bed of new potatoes and onions filled up a good portion of the left hand-side of the basement. Plenty of space was available.

At this point, I turned my attention to Sally, who said that she'd better be getting on home. "Bye, I've got to go. Momma will be wondering why I haven't come home for lunch."

"If you can come out tomorrow, we'll figure out when we'll start our school. I've got to hide the papers so you go on home."

I waved to Sally, and off she went. I could hear footsteps on the ceiling above me. I knew that I had better move quickly. Looking over the darkened basement, I decided to put my teaching materials back behind the canned tomatoes. No one would be going back there to get any until after school started in September because we saved them for when the garden played out.

"Momma, I'm hungry." I began climbing up the steps to the front porch where my mother sat stringing beans.

"Where have you been, young lady?"

"I've been with Sally."

"You must have been up to something because it's been awfully quiet around here."

Momma sat on the pale green porch-glider. Without taking her eyes off of me, she snipped off one end of a bean, first pulling the string and then snapping it into two pieces. She then tossed them into the waiting dishpan.

"Momma, Sally went home a few moments ago."

That was true even though I knew full well that I had not told the entire truth about the morning's events.

"Well, you better go on in the house and wash up. Your sister made lunch and we've already eaten. You help her with the dishes, then check on your baby sister. It's about time for her to wake up for her bottle. If you can be really quiet, you might first check on her and see if her diaper is dry. If it is, just let her sleep. Let me know if she needs changing. You can help me with feeding her when you are through with lunch."

"O.K. Momma, what's for lunch?"

I looked up at the yellow sticky fly-paper hanging from the porch's blue bead-board-ceiling. From where I stood, the fly-paper strips looked like they had black polka dots on them. Open doors and windows were an invitation!

"There's some macaroni and tomatoes, pinto beans and corn bread. You're lucky that your sisters and brother didn't eat it all up. Now go on, and get going. The day isn't getting any younger and I am going to need you to help me this afternoon."

I opened the screen door to the living room, walked into the kitchen where my sister was standing near the coal-fired stove. She put her finger to her lips and shushed me.

"I'm baking a cake. You've got to be quiet, or else, the cake will fall. You know what happened the last time."

A fallen cake tastes more like a cake that has turned into pudding. But not nearly as tasty as the banana pudding, full of vanilla wafers and sliced bananas that Momma makes. One has to be very careful not to slam doors, walk too heavily or run around when anything's in the oven. I tiptoed over to the stove and picked up my plate which was sitting on the warming shelf. I almost dropped it trying to avoid burning my arm as I reached over the stove top.

"Where've you been?"

"With Sally." I mumbled, swallowing a mouthful of food.

I tried to concentrate on eating my lunch. I was excited that I was going to get to be a teacher of my own classroom. I knew it would take some creative thinking to manage to avoid my bossy sister from ruining my plans.
	As the day winded down and I had finished my chores, I sat in the porch-swing and pondered how I would be able to find a way to go down to the basement and set up my classroom. Without anyone finding out. As it turned out, I did not have time to come up with a solution.

The next day there was a knock at the door.

I saw the pastor. Momma was standing in the living room with the baby in one arm as she opened the door with the other. There was no time to hide, no place to hide. No place to flee to, and just as quickly as I could even begin to think these thoughts, Momma came into the back bedroom, to where I was trying to make myself small.

"There's someone here to see you."

With Momma's assistance and encouragement, I went into the living room. My heart was thumping, wildly, in my ten-year old chest. My tongue was paralyzed.

"There seems to be many Sunday School materials missing from one of the classrooms. And, much to my dismay, I have discovered that there are pages missing from almost all of the hymnbooks. I am not asking if you know anything about it. What I would like to know is why you took them."

Now, how in the world had he found out? I was not about to ask him. But I sure was curious. I tried not to cry but the tears came. And that was before the spanking I knew was coming. My mother turned to me. "Why on earth did you tear out the pages from all of those hymnbooks?"

"It wasn't all my fault; Sally helped me."

I could not look at the pastor or my mother.

"You do know taking things that are not yours is wrong. It is a sin. You need to confess and ask for forgiveness. If you ever think of doing something that you do not want anyone to know about or if you are feeling you need to hide it, you will know that it is something you should not be doing in the first place. And, you really cannot hide it from God, because He knows everything."

If Sally ever got a good talking-to from her mother and the pastor like I did, I never knew. I knew she deserved it. After that incident, Sally and I seldom ever again played together. And only saw one another at the bus stop at the foot of the hill where my grandparents lived. Although, I never had heard of the term "grounded", I think we both were, forever, grounded from one another.

The hymn books had not remained in the same place from whence we had found them when we took possession of the pages. What a large amount of time and tape it took to put those pages back in the books! And, I had to save for months and months to reimburse my parents for the cost.

Each and every time I attended church, for years on end, I held a constant reminder in my hands of my crime. I had just as many years of confession and repentance as I sang hymns of praise and adoration. To his credit, Pastor continued to visit us at our home. He never brought the subject up to me again. He didn't have to do or say anything more. Each Sunday, I saw the taped pages in whatever hymnbook in whichever church pew I sat. They were vivid reminders of my transgression. They were also reminders of how I had been forgiven even when I did not deserve it.

Behind the Door

We talked about the olden days.
Days when we were young and untried.
Times when we went astray,
Not having a map to point the way.

We wandered as if in a dark forest, searching
For something more, searching for possibilities.

We walked about, with heads held high;
Thought we knew more than we actually did;
Believed to be wiser than we were;
Thought, if given a chance, an opportunity

We could have changed the world
At that very instant, and for the better.

We dreamed dreams without any idea
Of how to accomplish them,
Or what might be the cost, if by fate
Or effort, our dreams came true.

We wanted more than the status quo, more than
The circumstances in which we found ourselves.

Yet, an auspicious time arrived
When an awakening descended upon the town,
When educators, who, upon the end of the day,
Looked back and realized something was lacking,

Something more than living in the past
Where the present was the end of the road.

Jackie Davis Allen

Nightmare

Around her waist, an apron, its strings tied in the back.
Upon the apron sat a basket of ripened fruit, a peach
Oozed in her hand. And in the other, a knife,
Rounding the fruit's curves, exposing its sweet flesh.

Her birth name, unlike the fruit, was not yet of age.

Peaches was her little girl's name. She, early on,
Instructed in mountain ways, a lumberman's wife
Destined to be. She, learning her lessons earnestly.
Though, provocation prepared her not for the pain

That forever reminds her of the nightmare.

He, doting, seemed so kind, a hunting dog always
By his side, came upon her of a late morning, sitting
Out on porch; with hidden agenda, he was looking
To satisfy his thirst. And, the hunger of his greed,

Wanting, desiring a taste of something sweet.

He came alone that sunny day, just to sit and visit.
She, anxious for attention, not yet in her teens
Whose apron strings had not yet been cut. She
Unwittingly, innocently, accepted his invitation

And climbed up onto his blue-jean lap.

The dewy innocence of her rosy cheeks
Above her trembling cherry lips, quickly
Became dreadfully aware of something
Like fear arising, a dark terror descending.

No Illusions . . . *through the looking glass*

For, beneath, was a weapon,

Like a blade, pawing away at her resisting flesh.
Apron strings no longer a concern, innocence
Awakened, discarded, damaged, torn.
What a terrible bad dream!

Sadly soiled and sorrowfully stained, shaking,

With eyes downcast, she clambered down.
The morning basket of fruit tumbling.
The silver glint, now in hand,
Matched eyes of intent.

Both quivered at a sudden crackling sound.

It felled the nightmare down.
And, as Peaches looked on,
It is said, the sun smiled and the birds
Began to sing, once more.

Jackie Davis Allen

Think You upon This!

Anxiety ruled the days and nights.
The hours, waiting, were a trial
Against the time-worn clock, where
At the finish-line, the race over.
A winner chosen, and heart
Of hearts, something
Precious, endangered.

Steps, stairs, the course steep.
Both knees knocking,
Bereft of counsel, abandoned.
Hands rough and red, heart in hand,
Waiting, breathlessly. Then, the moment,
Finding voice, and wavering not,
I have not forgotten what I heard

Or, what was said.
Do as you please, for you will.
I have no other option
But to accede to your decision.
You deem me unfit, yet not one
Of you can attest to the legitimacy
Of the offense I am accused of.

What you choose to say or do
This day, this of all days
Will either elevate your name
Or taint both it and your fame.
Any blame rests
On your shoulders, not mine.
Think you now upon this!

Spirit-Song

A gentle wind, blowing, swirling.
I am embracing the day, my way.

My hair is tangled but I do not care.
I am sitting here on a mountain,
Near the edge of a steep cliff.

I like to secret myself in the mornings.
It is when I dig a bit deeper.

It is when I meditate, though tempted
To puncture the silence by singing.
I offer up a breath prayer, instead.

Burning brightly, the golden orb,
Comfortably rests in the arms of heaven.

And, against the azure blue, the beauty
And wonder of this place thrills me.
It fills me with its generosity and peace.

Jackie Davis Allen

Where There Is a Will . . .

Never had she seen the big city before,
Never ridden a bus
Where one had to cross the street
To catch the bus to return
From whence one had come.

She arrived from the mountains.
The land, scraped bare of coal, timber;
Where rains, flooding gorges, hollers,
Overflowed the banks;
Where people barely scraped by;

Where climbing up sliding mountains
And muddy hillsides, meant life or death,
The ravages of time and greed; where tears,
Storms and floods attempted
To wash away the stains,

The waters washed away homes,
Bridges, lives, hopes and dreams,
Stains of coal that no power
Could wash away; great anxiety
Like Black Lung, haunted their days.

The city offered hope, a promise, a ticket
Providing the means to escape poverty.
And on the wings of education, she would fly.
No matter which way the bus was going,
She would find her fortune there.

in the blink of an eye

the ticking of the clock silences her cry
squeezing tears from the slits
below her brow
claims a dream

and spins the curative dial
she, wagering against the diagnosis
of life, the fiber of her existence
against the azure blue
the evening, continuing its journey

from the eastern sky,
sailing across the pathway toward God
a shadow of simmering heat explodes
both her future

and her obscured prescience
the ticking of the clock spins,
echoes her pleading cries
and, suspended directly above her soul,
a prayer seeks a way to comprehend

sorrow, the inevitable,
finds its way ticking
against shimmering nights,
glides by even as life awaits

silently, stoically,
a commanding voice gradually
emerges from the shadows
as she lies down, it calls out *reply*
and the ticking clock blinks not its eye

Jackie Davis Allen

Tapestry

Looking through the mirror of time
Back into the quiet stirrings of Appalachia,
I see the twin mountains of want
And need, they, surrounding me

Silent echoes of memories and thoughts
Remind me of my innocence and passion,
My hunger for something more
Neither then wise nor knowledgeable

A half century ago, stifling screams
Of protest, with no place to go, I dreamed
Of a world beyond the twin mountains
Both which protected and imprisoned

A dichotomy of a time when innocence
Was valued by country, church and family
And by those bent on exploitation
To satisfy their own greed and lust

Survival, the instinct of living, living
Beyond the moment, arms clinging
To the hope of something more,
I made mistakes, yet I persevered

autumn's chill

the silvery moon spilled its magic
onto the mirrored face
of the lake
like a lingering kiss,
I will always remember
the dark limbs, the nearby trees
rattling their aged bones
and in the icy breeze, transfixed,
I shuddered to think
was it just yesterday
when, within the recesses
of my being, I promised
never again, never
would I return
to the lake forlorn
and yet here I stand,
remembering the weight
of the past, the incredible weight
of the haunting shadows
rippling across the face
of the mirrored lake
remembering still, when
with Father Time standing idly by
sweet summer breathed her last
and of autumn's icy chill
and her embrace? well,
it remains with me still

Jackie Davis Allen

O Lord, Have Mercy!

Standing on the porch looking down on the
Road. I see before me, life
Passing by. Ponderous coal trucks huffing
And puffing, as they transport loads
To the railroad cars, waiting down by the depot.

Lying in the bedroom. Looking up at the
Ceiling. Uncle coughs, barely
Breathing. Tethered to a tank whose
Tube extends his life twenty-four hours
A day, seven days a week. All year long.

Working in the kitchen,
Auntie stirs a pot of greens
With an eye on the soup beans,
The other hawk-eye on the oven-window
Where, behind, bakes corn bread.

It is a miner's wife's rendition of a gourmet meal.

Crying in Granny's tired arms,
Seven months-old Johnny,
Unable to be consoled. His colic rises up
And violently vacates his vitality.
The heaving of his chest

Causes all of us to break out in prayer.

O, the woes of a coal miner's family!
Mine, theirs, yours, ours, we struggle
To make ends meet. Even when there's little
To stretch a meal, we invite strangers
To come sup with us.

And please, do take a seat!

No Illusions . . . *through the looking glass*

With heads bowed, we offer up a prayer
The little ones may mumble using what
Communication skills they have
And with their eyes tightly closed,
We hear them saying at the end,

"God bless, and Amen!"

Falling into my shared bed,
The floor creaks, then relaxes
While I chase white counting-sheep
And pray to sleep, pleading with God
To make things right, that

Johnny and uncle will survive the night.

Jackie Davis Allen

Lonely

He knew not what they thought
He was but a young teen
The room, the space, the air
The same everywhere

Silent as the grave
Whenever he appeared
And still he sought
Hoping, praying

To understand
His heart heavy, longing
What more it was,
Unsure, uncertain,

He could do to prevent
Being ignored, ridiculed
To help them comprehend
They, disinterested, self-absorbed,

Unknowing, uncaring, unaware
That all he wanted from them
With every fiber of his being
Was to be their friend

But then, time,
Like hope,
Was running out
For him

No Illusions . . . through the looking glass

One of a Kind

Crawling, tottering, running, struggling
Diligently searching for her pot of gold
She fell from exhaustion, the getting up
And falling down requiring too much effort
Though she persevered until the end

Drained like a creek run dry, she prayed
That if and when she found her rainbow
She'd have the desire and energy, it to claim
She'd begin all over again, God willing,
And she'd not sink back down into the darkness

I still hear her laughter, see the brilliance
Behind her eyes, behind her smile
Yet in the distorted mirror of self-reflection
That keeps one awake at night
She'd seen only a ghost of herself

Self-talk placed perfection at the top
Of her list, blinded her ability to understand
That she was more than what she thought
She, needing more than love can give, feeling
As if she were fighting the battle alone

Remembering with sweet sorrow
The season of her fragrance, like a rare rose,
Treasured, pressed down between the pages
I shall always keep her in my heart and mind
She was a most beloved friend, one of a kind

Jackie Davis Allen

A Turn in the Road

Walking by your house
The lights no longer on
I think of you, the two of us
Moments of intimacy

Forever, I think
They will be a part of my heart

The nights are dark, long
And still your house I pass by, hoping
To see your car in the driveway

My mind revisits, too
The things we used to do

Moments spent cuddling
Dancing, talking, loving
They, dissipating now
Into the mist of heartache

For months, I have heard nothing
Not one word from you

Was there something I said
Or did, or did not do?
Should I pick up the phone?
Yes, that is just what I will do!

Garden of Dreams

He tended the garden, cultivated
Its promise, cared for its fruit,
Cultivated its potential
She, the intention of his love
And abiding faithfulness

She thrived on his generosity,
Love and attention
Until blossoming
Lush and ripened, she climbed
Over the vine of time

At the peak of her beauty,
Anticipating an invitation,
She nodded her head
To dine in the union
He had carefully designed

Jackie Davis Allen

Revision Quest

Scanning the scene, I discovered a book
Its cover, plastered
In high relief, surreal in nature
On the landscape were shadows,
Embedded ferociously
In the heart of Main Street
Wailing, a flashing strobe
Reflected a stethoscope
And as if it were painted with dread
Throbbing shades of pain's
Malfeasance stained the cover, bluish black
Praying the script's demise
Did not include me, I attempted
To remain incognito, my efforts consigned
To playing the part of a survivor
Who overcomes fear
Beating erratically, my heart skipped a beat
A steel door opened as if by magic
Before me, glancing right
And left, with hands groping,
Stood one cloaked in ancient garb
And, lying on the table, my pen
Cold and sterile, I hoped
It was not too late for me, perhaps,
Even a few moments early
With eyes opened, I claimed the pen,
Seized its availability and began to surgically
Examine my choices. I can write
Or I can do nothing and let my gift die

The Winter of His Age

Snow's white
Crowns his head
As before me he sits

The fire
Of expectation
Flickers gently
Like a candle

The candle's wick
Has been trimmed
One too many times

And, in the mirror
Of his past,
It greets him
As a youth

In consolation
For memory lost,
It returns him to the cradle

Where he is playing
With its shadow
And now
With stumbling steps

Fumbling, he is searching
For the little
Of the light that remains

On the Other Hand

Every day it happened.
One blow after another.
His anger flashed hot like a spiraling siren.
It wrapped its harm around her innocence.
It beat its repetitive rhythm into her brain.

Every time the strobes
Of his sneering right, flashed bright,
Breathed raw with blood against her lips,
Blackened her eyes with the shame of his blame,
It tarnished her dignity. She, but a tortured trophy.

As always, his anger muscled
Its prowess. Self-righteously, it reigned
Supreme, claimed as sole right its will
Over her, the right to enter, to knock or not.
It reduced her to less than a soiled doormat.

Searing hot, the wounds infected.
They rendered her unable
To endure the pain that hovered
Over the cracked mirror that
Reflected, confirmed her desperation.

Like a ticking clock, years
Of pulsating wounds painted her nights,
Her days, her existence as bleak
As the tomorrows she feared never to come:
A nightmare singing its own song

Every day.

Until one day . . .

Happy Birthday to Me

Our family was not wealthy, by any standards. However, I'm sure many must have thought we were. You see, Poppa had a car. And, some other things that were gifts from one of his sisters, the one who was an antique dealer.

Actually, our family was pretty much isolated from the rest of the county, sandwiched in-between the many mountain ridges. We had no television, no telephone, nor any magazines. Yet, life was pretty good, if you didn't consider that there wasn't always enough to eat. Hand-me-downs were expectantly appreciated when another of Poppa's sisters arrived with her car, filled with surprises.

It was especially good when Grandpa's check came in. With it, he allowed us to dream dreams we could never ever could have hoped to come true. He'd say, "Get out the 'Wish Book' and have your Momma send me the bill."

Sears Roebuck, Montgomery Ward, and Alden's were where our dreams were circled in on the various pages, as in, *this, I'd like to have and that, too*. And, maybe, I'll mark this as first choice and that one, second choice. Always knowing it was a pretend-game and that one couldn't count on dreams coming true. But, sometimes they did.

Grandpa gave me a doll for my birthday. Momma and Poppa gave me a yellow dress. The tag on the package, wrapped in newspaper, said, "From Momma and Poppa".

My dress matched the one the doll was wearing.

The Colors We Wear

It all began when I surreptitiously climbed upon the first shelf, then the second shelf. You might ask why I was doing that? I was trying to reach the forbidden top shelf of my mother's kitchen cabinet. That's where the object of my attention was supposed to be. I'd seen Momma put it there, high and away from my prying eyes.

But, there at the top, hidden behind a vase of fading silk flowers, was the tin can. Mustard-yellow in color. It held the largess of her savings. Mostly coins paid to her in appreciation for some kindness she had provided to those less fortunate than herself.

There was this lady named Mrs. Jones. She asked of my mother a favor. She was a widow. Her girth was so large it strained the frame of the doorway when she entered or exited a room. She had to turn herself sideways to do either. It was both sad, and pathetically, comical.

It was she who begged my mother to fashion her a dress. From a feed-sack, no less. Never mind that the poor scrap of fabric presented to my mother was imprinted with the logo that fed the chickens. Or, that the yardage was so small it would neither wrap around her waist nor cover her ample bosom. Or her bottom.

"A lesson in charity," my Momma explained, when I asked her, "How can you make anything from that?"

Momma took some time before she continued. Understand, she was never one to be deterred from a mission. As usual, Momma determined that Mrs. Jones and her situation had been handed to her, directly from God. There she goes with her, "Where's there's a will, there's a way."

"It was God himself who told me that I must do everything I can for Mrs. Jones. Who else has a sewing machine and the skill to work such a miracle?"

No Illusions . . . *through the looking glass*

I can say that I, myself, never actually heard God speak, but Momma said he talked to her. And if she said so, then it must be so. I'm still waiting for God to speak to me. Whether in regards to the farm, the house, the cooking, manners, schooling, or charity, Momma regarded "slacking off" as sinful. She smiled her "Wherever there's a will"-smile. And, figuratively, if not literally, she rolled up her sleeves and began to take some measurements. In the days that followed, and with missionary-like zeal, Momma took on the task of making Mrs. Jones a dress.

Momma never wasted a scrap of fabric. From her quilting scrap-bag, she began to pull out some of the largest pieces. Putting them together with the feed-sack bag Mrs. James gave her, she began to stitch her way toward yards and yards of material, piecing them together in ways that were magical. One strip was but two inches wide, a robin's egg-blue background upon which white roosters with red combs strutted. She stitched this strip adjacent to a strip made of brick-like blocks, yellow with purple polka dots.

Next to it, she stitched up some green striped scraps, interspersing them with solid orange pieces. Another larger scrap of fabric, perhaps a quarter yard wide, held bouquets of white flowers. They sat on a bed of pink cups and saucers, with teapots dancing around the selvages. Although, most of the fabric scraps Momma used were no more than two to three inches wide, she managed to make something beautiful. Of course, I knew it was a gift she had been given: making something from nothing. Momma had a picture in her head.

The scraps of fabric came from all kinds of different places, states and towns, hollers and who knows where else. The word had gotten around. If anyone had a piece of fabric they had no use for, they knew who to give it to. My Momma. She married all those little pieces to each other in such a way that their disparate parts would have even found the pastor preaching on "Momma's Miracle" had he been aware of it in the making.

As she busied herself, Momma hummed, and sang. Mostly *Amazing Grace, How Sweet the Sound.* She, in her nasal twang, sang the song over and over until I, myself had it memorized. In the end, she had fashioned six yards of what she called "patchwork". And, then, she started over again, giving no never mind as to whether or not the "patchwork" matched the feed-sack scrap that Mrs. Jones had handed her. It was little more than the size of a dishrag. Nothing was going to stand in Momma's way.

If you've not already sensed it, Momma was determined to fulfill the merging dream the two women shared, for Mrs. Jones to have a second dress to wear. I can't remember my mother ever receiving much more than a "Thank you" for her sacrificial efforts and designing skill. Sometimes, she'd be paid a hundred pennies, or perhaps as little as two quarters. Or, as Mrs. Jones would say, "Is two bits enough?" I think that meant two quarters. Regardless, it would not pay for thread, buttons, zippers, and any lace or trim Momma decided to use.

And, of course, I stood by, rolling my disrespectful eyes, unable to conceal my disbelief, yet knowing that my mother would smilingly nod her head and say, "Yes, I think that will do just fine."

That tin can was my undoing. It was a mustard-yellow can, the kind that held the makings used to make mustard plasters for whatever ailed you. I coveted the money in it. Coveted means I wanted it. I really, really wanted it. What I'd spend it on, or where, or how I'd explain my sudden wealth, I never gave that any consideration.

As I said at the beginning, I climbed up the first two shelves, the first two steps to where I thought I would find the treasure containing the coins. Great wealth untold was just a reach away. Instead, I succumbed into oblivion as the kitchen cabinet toppled over on top of me. It smashed the living daylights out of my larcenous thoughts, the coins scattering. I have no recollection of anything other than the room going dark. Two days later, with a sick, throbbing headache, I woke up, only to be told, and not in any uncertain terms, "Young lady, you're lucky to be alive."

Right then and there I decided I'd go straight. I'd try to mend my ways. I'd try to match my thoughts to more charitable ones. Like those of my mother. And, I made it my solemn promise, both to Momma and to God. I made the promise silently, just in case I might forget and backslide. I didn't always remember to follow up.

Mrs. Jones, true to my reckoning, when the dress was finished, paid my mother the "two bits". That is a measly fifty cents. The dress, large, was beautiful, with colors as bold and as amazing as Joseph's Coat of Many Colors. It must have been so. Momma loved making people happy.

When Mrs. Jones saw her dress, the smile on her face was as delightful as was the twisting and twirling dance she performed before Momma's rounded art-nouveau mirror. I thought, if she gets dizzy, we will have to have uncle come out with his truck and take her to the hospital. But, how would we get her up into the truck bed? Poppa had a jack he used to lift the house up, so as to put cinderblocks underneath it. Somehow, I didn't think that would work.

Thank goodness, she didn't fall. Mrs. Jones and Momma were as happy as two peas in a pod, both of them relishing in the miracle of the dress. Where the feed-sack fabric was, well, one would have had to have search long and hard to find it. I declare, Mrs. Jones and Momma's smiles were almost as wide as Mrs. Jones' backside.

Sorry, I shouldn't have said that, but I just couldn't resist.

Her daughter-in-law, parked outside of our house, came up the steps just about then and ushered Mrs. Jones and her miracle dress toward her station wagon. I waved as they pulled off onto the road and began their trip home. Momma'd be basking in the glory for months, or at least until she heard the voice of God giving her yet another invitation to do his bidding.

Jackie Davis Allen

Promises, Colors and Coupons

Funny how things stick in one's mind. Things that should, don't. Things that shouldn't, do. Seems like it always happens that way with me.

Of course, I didn't write all this down at the time that it all happened. You'll just have to pardon me if I fill in some of the blanks and blame it on the lump I got on my head that day when the cabinet fell on top of me.

It's most curious, how, when I went through the lunch line at school, I avoided the bananas. The color yellow reminded me that I had made a promise to walk a straight and narrow line as far as getting into trouble. Oh, I know, bananas don't have anything to do with the greed my heart had held for Momma's mustard-jar money. Somehow, though, that yellow fruit was like a signpost, saying, "You promised, and you know that God knows everything".

Well, I always knew that. I wasn't stupid. But I will hand you this, in the midst of getting into trouble, I always seemed to have a problem with remembering about the promises I'd previously made.

As the years went by, my phobia with the color yellow dissipated. Dissipated. A beautiful word! In fact, I grew to love the color of bananas.

I studied a lot and learned more and more. And, I got interested in reading the dictionary. Oh, yes! In our home, we had no television, just the radio to catch up on the news of what was going on in the world. And, two books, the Bible and Webster's Dictionary. Listening to Big Ben at night, before going to bed, my ear pressed up against the radio. Well, now, that was a novelty. I imagine you can rightly understand how the dictionary might have been a tool to discovering some ways to entertain myself. Eventually, however, I tired of that.

One day, my grandmother called out to me. She stood on the far corner of her wrap-around porch and yelled. I was standing on my own front porch, not a wrap-around one like hers. I could hear her real well. Grandma's voice carried through the air. I suppose that's because she lived high up on top of the hill and we lived beyond, below.

"I've got some Coca Cola bottles. You can have them. Check with your Momma before you come on out."

What exciting news! I knew if and when I got some money where I could now spend it. Up the road, around the winding, switch-back curves was a small store. The facade was so dark it looked like the bark of the oldest tree I'd ever seen. Like the logs down at the sawmill waiting to be made into boards. I liked that word. It was as if it was something that a Parisian might say. Of course, I'd never been out of the county, not to mention the country.

    My father promised, if ever he got off the midnight shift, and if he ever got a few days off from the mines, he'd take us to Florida. Ah, Florida! The land of sunshine, blue skies, the ocean, beach and palm trees. And, bananas, oranges, grapefruit, lemons, limes. It was a dream I held close to my heart. I prayed that somehow God would work a miracle and it would be so. It would be so wonderful.

    Anyway, I had a coupon. The librarian at school, in exchange for my helping her, had given me some old magazines. Yellowed and dog-eared were the pages, but inside, I discovered coupons! Never had I known that something like that could be cut out and exchanged for candy, ice cream, and more. I didn't bother to ask Momma, and went to Grandma's and picked up the coke bottles. I had to be careful carrying them down the hill where I placed them in my little wagon. Momma was in the garden and would be for some time. She wouldn't even know I was gone. So, I carted the coke bottles up the road, they, rattling in the wagon. I parked my wagon outside and the storekeeper came out to check how many bottles I had. A penny for each bottle exchanged, and with five cents for the coke bottles, I gave the pennies along with the coupon to the clerk. He was also the owner. "I'll have that ice cream." I pointed to the one in the cooler that was sandwiched between two chocolate cookies.

I know I'm supposed to respect my elders. After all, my eye rolling-days should have been over. But I simply couldn't understand how a tiny little printed date of just a few days ago could be an obstacle between what I saw in the ice cream case and having it in my hands.

"Just this one time, and never again. I'm going to give you the ice cream even though the coupon has expired. So, don't ever come back here with a request like that again, or else, I'll tell your parents."

The ice cream sandwich bar was good. I didn't dare tell Momma for fear I'd have to tell her about my being disrespectful and for arguing with the store keeper. I just couldn't understand why the storekeeper had to make such a fuss over a couple of days. I was smart enough to know that I didn't want to tangle with my parents, regardless of how ridiculous I thought the matter was. He had plenty more ice creams in that refrigerated case. But I figured it'd be a good idea not to test him again.

The sun seemed always hesitant to move from the east and on over across the railroad tracks, the creek, the road and settle down around our house. It hid behind the mountain until it got tired of being in the shadows. Then, around noon, it seemed to reach out and grab hold of the side of the mountain where we lived. And, there, for the first time of the day, I saw the golden orb. It sat directly overhead.

"Orb." Now there's a word for you! Golden orb, the sun.

If I ever got another chance to help the librarian out, and if she ever gives me anymore magazines, I'll remember to check out the expiration date on those coupons. I get into enough trouble on my own. I don't need any extra help.

No Illusions . . . through the looking glass

Hope

The sun is shining its smile this morning.
A cold and brisk breeze is blowing.
And, as I sit here, still sad and blue, and unknowing
What it is that I'm supposed to do with the letter
In my pocket, written from me to you.
Should I post it, or forgetting, should I burn it
And just try to live as if nothing had ever happened?

The rain is falling, midst clouds, dark and gray.
My heart is throbbing, a pain that won't go away.
The doctor said that daily exercise might help.
But my, or my, what do I do during the night
When tears flood my pillow, and memories without sleep
Threaten to exhaust me? I wonder if ever our love
Will keep, or has it been strained by the stain.

Snow is blowing its icy white, laying down its coat
While the candle of my heart flickers with hope.
And, should fate allow, I pray the music
Of my heart's drum might be one most pleasing
To you, for my most earnest desire
Is to give myself entirely up to your keeping.
The clock has ticked away, so too, our song.

Another letter, I must write, some things I must share.
Some of my longing, some of the misery, the anguish
Of what I have been through, though no words
Are sufficient to explain the pain of having not heard
Even one word from you, my heart's desire.
The sun is shining, a storm is brewing.
And I, sit here, alone, beneath a sad and blue omen.

Wishful Thinking

A young girl, craving romance
A beau and a chance to attend a dance
Dreams of a slinky evening-gown
Filled out, in all of the right places
With pink rosebuds encircling her wrist

Alas, it is but a black and white dream

As in a fairy tale, one auspicious day
A young man, from a higher class
Knocks on the door, invites her
To say yes, to accompany him
To the dance, that very same night

In her wildest dreams, never such a fantasy

As obedient daughter, reluctantly acquiescing
She hopes to make of herself a willing date
Attired in a silken gown of prettiest pink
She smiles all during his neglect
Considers his inexperience, counts up the cost

His peers surely will exact for his loss

The band plays on, all the other couples dance
On the sidelines, the pink one, a flower, wilting
Weighs, she, the circumstances of the scene
Both he and she, on the threshold of discovering
That wishful thinking requires effort to bloom

First Love

His presence caused the essence
Of romance to color my days.
It seemed it was his intent
Any fears, of mine, to allay.

As suitor, he was quite smart,
Showering on me his utmost attention.
Though, in truth, on my part,
Some apprehension I did discern.

Yet, for the sake of my heart, it I ignored.
He went away. He left me high and dry.
He was the one who set my heart a' pitter-patter
And caused the song birds to scatter.

For when first we did meet,
My heart skipped a couple of beats
And heavenly wings, mysteriously
Did appear upon my feet.

With youthful buds of desiring
And with sparks of love igniting
The stage for romance was aflame.
Passion consumed our nights.

Now, my days are filled with despair.
He extinguished any thoughts of delight.
He went away. Oh why? Oh why
Did he leave me high and dry?

Jackie Davis Allen

The Night-Visitors

I was lying in my bed that night, with my bedroom door open. I could see diagonally into the living room and its front door. The door that had a window, so we could see whoever it was that had come to visit.

I had difficulty sleeping back then. My bedtime ritual of saying goodnight put the Walton's to shame, mine more plentiful. I hoped that there would be no response when I said goodnight to my parents, individually, and to my siblings, individually. If they did not respond, that meant they were asleep and I could go to sleep. Why did I feel I had to stay awake? My agitated parents did not understand.

"If you say goodnight one more time, you'll be sorry. Go to sleep!"

Many a long night, I laid in my bed, listening to every sound, wondering what it might be, and wondering if ever I would fall asleep. Counting sheep and repeating every prayer I knew, and some of my own, probably kept me awake as much as did my constant companion, insomnia. Ah, the workings of a young mind!

My parents' bedroom was just steps away from the living room. My own bedroom was at the back side of the house, where, I told you already, I had an angled view into the living room. Poppa was supposed to have been in Georgia where he had gone to buy peaches. He and a neighbor had gone there to bring back home the fresh fruit which Momma would can so that we would have it for the wintertime. For some reason, which I have long forgotten, he came back from Georgia a day early. But under the cover of the dark.

Tired from the long trip, Poppa decided to wait until morning to unload the peaches. Knowing full well that if he parked his truck in its usual place, across the road from our house, the peaches would long be gone before morning. He asked one of Momma's relatives, who lived across the road, across the creek, and below the railroad tracks, if he might park his truck at her house. This neighbor agreed that it would be fine. Poppa's truck would not be visible from the road and the peaches would be safe.

In our roadside neighborhood, everyone knew everyone and everyone knew everyone else's business. I sometimes thought they knew my business before I even knew it. The absence of Poppa's truck indicated to all that he was still in Georgia, and definitely not home.

So much that happens in our lives gets forgotten. As a result, part of history disappears. While I am still able to remember, I want to share now what happened that night, more than a half century ago. Anyone who is unfamiliar with the life and times of living in an isolated, rural and mountainous area might better understand how our home was an easy target for any prowler-seeking mischief. If they but realized that there were no streetlights, no sidewalks and no telephones. The police station was seventeen miles away, across winding and treacherous mountainous roads.

As the darkness descended, engulfing the mountains, I heard nothing but hushed breathing, rhythmically rising and falling. My family was asleep. And I, counting sheep, was unable to match the rise and fall of their silent breaths. Sleep failed me. Why did sleep come so easily to others?

The moon and stars watched over this midnight-mystery, while I lay, praying for release from the dark and ominous fears that wandered through my mind. My breathing came faster as danger loomed in the shadows at the front door. Whoever could it be? And, at this time of the night? And, whatever could they be wanting? I listened to every creaking, crackling sound that dared to step outside of the quieter and more steadily breathing sounds of my entire sleeping family. My heart beat so loud it echoed in my ears. I heard voices. The drumming of my pulse issued a warning. I was afraid.

Danger had stolen my breath and had rendered my legs unsteady, so I crawled toward my parents. I struggled to breathe, yet tried to hold my breath. At the same time, I wondered if this was why insomnia had sought me out. Fear overtook my body as I crawled on my shaking knees, coming nearer to my parents' bedroom. I woke Poppa up. He was annoyed and, not sensing the truth of my desperation, ordered me back to my bed. I tried again, but he needed his sleep. "It's just a bad dream."

If only that had been true. The images behind those shadows were only too real. Disappointed, and still on bended knees, not reassured, and with my heart thumping, tears silently streaming, throat constricted, I began crawling back to my bedroom, fearfully aware that danger still lurked. Where were they now? And who were they?

Returning to bed, nearly paralyzed from fright, on that warm summer night, danger had revealed men's faces, their intent concealed by the night. And I was, yet again, on the floor crawling toward my parents' bedroom, praying that the night would cover me with a blanket of safety, of invisibility. And, that my father would believe me. Persevering, I crawled faster, knees having traced this same path before. Adrenalin pumping, body exhausted, heart thumping, ears ringing, I opened my mouth, determined to survive, the words coming out in hoarse spurts.

My shaken father, now trusting and believing, got up out of bed and took his shotgun from the closet. Through the living room door, he exited out into the darkness of the night. The men were outside the window which was at the foot of my bed. My siblings remained unaware, asleep. With a determined and firm stance, my father shouted out a warning. He aimed his gun and the blast that pierced the night echoed off the sides of the mountain.

My heart continued its thumping, racing with my rasping breath. My fear subsided a little when the prowling young men ran from the side of my house, across the road, across the creek, across the railroad tracks. Finally, they scrambled up the hill just below my great aunt's house. They were grabbing handfuls of dirt and attempting to climb up the mountain in an effort to hide and escape my father's judgment. The moon was the spotlight that brought it all into view. The men escaped and we were safe. No one was struck by the blast from Poppa's gun.

A patrol car came by later that night, while Poppa was still outdoors with his shotgun. He flagged the policeman down, told him what had happened. And if any of those men were ever caught, I never heard tell of it.

Morning came, and I was exhausted.

Jackie Davis Allen

Christmas Eve

The stockings are hanging from the mantle.
Each is red and labeled with a particular name,
With love, care, filled to the top. Not one, the same.

Gifts, gaily wrapped in colored papers, beneath
The tree, silently wait for the moment
Of expected excitement and joyous merriment.

Shiny ornaments are hanging on the tree's branches.
Some new, some old, and some quite antique,
With interesting stories, if only they could speak.

The tree lights are clear, shining ever so brightly.
They reflect the glory of that long-ago night
When a baby was born, Jesus was his name.

An angel, on top of the tree, holds a lighted candle,
A symbol of one who announced the birth
Of the promised one, come to earth.

Praises of adoration and honor to him belong.
The wrappings, the ribbons, and even the songs
Represent the joy we share by giving to others.

The night is called Christmas by those who believe.
It represents not the date, but the birth of a king.
May we rejoice as we sing Merry Christmas to all!

The Night Before Last

The baby was finally tucked in her bed, asleep like an angel, golden curls surrounding her head. Not a peep did I hear. So, I knew I had nothing to fear. The icing, made, the cookies waiting on a plate. And I, still in my apron, cleared off the table, placed the cookies by the fireplace in the hope that Santa would come and make himself at home. I wondered if my adventurous daughter would awaken during the night and eat them up.

The sight of the cookies and my aching back told me it was time to join my husband and go to bed. A few whispers, a couple of hugs, a kiss on his cheek and I knew very soon we'd both be fast asleep. The house was quiet, a little creaking, here and there as it cooled off. The coals in the cookstove were tiring, yielding the last of their heat. I went to check on little Molly, hoping to find her still asleep.

To my utter surprise, she was gone! Molly was not in her bed. The bed clothes were rumpled, the pillow askew, but where ever could she be? I checked the front door. It was still locked. Concerned that she might be in the kitchen, I peeped around the corner, and to my shock, my latent fears were realized. Molly was standing before me, covered from head to toe with dark chocolate syrup. I picked up my slimy and sticky little girl, tried my best not to smile nor to cry as I wiped away a curl that had stuck to her right eye.

The tepid bathwater turned a murky and funny shade of brown as I bathed my darling three-year-old, from the top of her little head down to her wiggly toes. She giggled and smiled, melting my heart. I smiled as I thought of the fun she must have had transforming herself into a gooey mess.

Jackie Davis Allen

Intercession

Admonish him, O Conscious!
For he, having gone his own way,
Has, from pride's accolade, not abided
By your most wise and high counsel.

He has coveted the lush fruit
Of duty's effort, yet he has tasted not
The bounty of the field's wanting labor.
He has laid waste to his self-worth.

O, worrisome weeds of woe's discontent,
Germinate neither his selfsame seeds
Nor paint his feet with jealousy's greed!
For I fear his eventual fall from grace.

May he, anew, still rise up in denial
Of self, and may the sweet bread
Of understanding fill his hunger.
Pray that his progeny be so inclined!

Absolve his shame, O Merciful One!
Grant that his cup of thirst be filled
With love and forgiveness! And, may
His life's purpose be a blessing.

A Night Filled with Choices

Brilliant city lights, splendiferous
Impassioned nights, precipitous
Filled with alluring excitement
Anticipating, considering possibilities

Seductive, she pondered her response
To the young man with flashing eyes
The one with the mysterious smile
And decided upon a plan

Like bees attracted to pollen
Indulgently, like bees to honey
Innocently, she desired
To offer her charms, exchanging them

For the chance to dance
To the music and to the beat
She smiled at him
And he began to shuffle his feet

Attracted by his mysterious smile
And by his shuffling feet
She caught his eye. He caught hers
And the music faded into the night

Jackie Davis Allen

House on the Hill

Perched high on stilts, a rickety old house
Barely stands. It looks distraught, unkempt
Leaning dangerously against the hill
Beneath a ghostly gathering of clouds

Breathes now, a deep sigh of despair
Blinded are the windows of its eyes
And approaching, a fierce storm rages
Mournful cries begin to surge

The house creaks with the wind, and ravens
With wings eerily silent and heavily still
Guard the old stone wall, wings folded
As if in prayer, they strut back and forth

Time wraps its arms around the old house
The vigilant ravens, in contemplation
Release their harsh cries as if from generations
They are witnessing history for the first time

The old house seems ever more the pitiful
It is but a shadowed-reminder of the past
And of its long-ago, no-more inhabitants
The house is weighed down by absence

The old house creaks, leans, groans, and
Expressing its final farewell, with a thud
It falls, becoming one with the hill, lifeless
Silent, asleep beneath the pale moon

The Survivors

Loss of communion with family
Friends, injured, captured, bled
Midst hailstorm, some spirits
Faltered, drifted, toppled
As did some of their own kind.

On land, on sea, as far away as the stars
Pardon served little comfort
For those left behind
Who pray tell, if they survive
Will be tomorrow's descendants.

They came to fight, to engage
Trained by listed numbers
Some died, infected with ideals
Each chose sides, waved colors
Some trampled them through the mud.

Long served some their country
Long suffered they the distance
Some were dreamers, some with old dreams
Shall insight, then, offer hope and promise
To those who survive the confrontation?

Jackie Davis Allen

Reflections

There is no way that my parents could have been able to fathom what lay ahead of them back in the early 1940s, or, for that matter, what lay ahead for me, their second eldest child. When they met and consummated their love, in the coalfield area of West Virginia, the United States and their Allies were waging the Second World War.

As I grew older, with questions, much of what I asked my parents about that time remains, to this day, unanswered. As a child I could not understand why they only smiled and shook their head, saying, "I'm busy. Go play."

During the time my father was in North Africa, serving as an ammunition carrier, I was born. Later, he showed me a picture of a chubby six-month-old with long dark hair. Pointing to the frayed and worn, black and white photograph, he told me, "That's you. I carried this picture of you underneath my hat and brought it back home." I do not recall puffing out my chest, but I imagine that I did something like that, in delight, though little realizing the significance of what a miracle it was that Poppa had, indeed, returned home. With no obvious battle wounds.

Poppa, a coal-miner, was slim and wiry, and around five and a half-foot tall. And, how I delighted in the pleasure that I had been named after him. Never did I consider him anything other than a strong man. He'd smile when I asked him, "Poppa, what did you do in the war?" Avoiding the question, he'd look away and continue to smile as he cleaned his prized trophies, guns and swords. Somehow, he managed to send them back to Momma before the war was over.

When I was around 10 years old, and wearing my blue jeans, handed down from a distant male cousin, I walked out onto our front porch, and seeing Poppa standing there with his thumbs stuck down in either pocket of his jeans, I struck a similar pose. I fancied myself even looking like him. Such was my attachment with my father that I intensely disliked housework. I chose to be with him whenever I could. Washing the car, laying pipe for our newly-dug well, working in the yard, and even taking up for him when he cut down Momma's flowers with the rotary push lawnmower.

"They were in the way," I explained.

For a time, before Poppa came home from the war, my Momma and my older sister lived with Momma's parents. During that time, my grandparents still had six children living at home. Their small four room house sat perched upon a hill with a narrow winding road down below. Surrounded by mountains on either side of the road, they were blessed to have a stream of water running down below their yard. It provided cool and refreshing waters to supplement their outdoor hand-pump, and the washing, done by hand on the washboard, come laundry-day.

    I cannot imagine how long it might have been before Momma decided, or perhaps was invited, to return to West Virginia to live with one of Poppa's sisters and her husband. Even still, I was born at the old hospital, over at the county seat, just a mile or so from the old town of Grundy, which was later torn down due to the ravages of decades of flooding. Only the old Court House remains.

    Unfortunately, there is no one living that can provide or confirm any information as to the timeline when my Momma and my two sisters and I moved from one place to another, until the time when Poppa was living in the hospital apartment building. It took some time for my fear, the one that had me crawling across my aunt's kitchen floor, faded into the past. However, it followed me until I was around ten or so when Grandpa would take me up into the mountains, high up, where his fields were located. He had many garden plots up there, and each one, planted with a single crop of corn, tomatoes, potatoes, and onions, separated by a long distance. Or so it seemed to my short and young legs.

    While standing on the road down below my

grandparents' house, I could see the incline of the carved out-path which the mule and its cart took when Grandpa led them up to tend his fields. Today, that path is abandoned, obscured by trees that have grown up to kiss the sky. For a time, he would let me ride in the wooden cart on its way up. On the way down, I had to gingerly make my way, lest I rolled down the hill like the marble on my aunt's kitchen-floor. Grandpa would fill his cart with fertilizer, hoes, and baskets on the way up. And, filled it with garden produce on the way down.

There was no place left for me. So, I walked behind.

A Breakthrough

I will write and write and compose
Until I cannot write anymore
Of the brick walls, the obstacle kind
I never have been, nor am I a fan.

Yet, I am sorely plastered up
Against the difficult task
Of either breaking through
Or climbing over that troublesome wall.

My masterpieces find their way
Into the bottom of wastebaskets
Crumpled up, stained, discarded
Most likely misunderstood.

However, providentially, probably
Because I have eyes with which to see
And mind and heart with which to believe
I retrieve the sheets, reverently.

Smoothing them out, gingerly
Taking pity, I recast them artfully
Into a new and better light, they
With musical refrains, delightfully sweet.

Even the piano keys begin to dance
Trembling with energy that competes
With my soloing fingers, tap dancing
Against the background of the morning.

Jackie Davis Allen

At My Window

Dampened spirits
Driving rain
Sea and sand
Wind and ocean
Howling
Growling
Sitting here
Thinking

This was supposed
To be my vacation

Embracing the Gift

This gift that I have lies dormant within,
Hoping one day to find expression.
I rehearse my plan over and over
Until I am stressed out,
With no release. Gift's frustration.

You are my love, or once you were.
What happened is that fear grew,
Intimidation took its place,
With dreams unfulfilled and extinguished.
Will hope rekindle gift's potential?

This gift that I have, now expressed
From within, splashes upon the canvas
Until, with paint and brush,
I am exhausted, an image incomplete,
Still unfinished, filled with desire.

You are my love, and still are.
The seed of desire emerges, leaping
Over hurdles, ignoring intimidation
And picking up the brush again,
Dipping into paint, love's gift reawakens.

This gift that I have joyfully finds
Expression with bursts of exuberant color
Across and within the canvas of life.
Embracing the gift, I am motivated
Once again to dance, to paint, to create.

Jackie Davis Allen

Birds of a Different Feather

Hiding behind web-like corridors
Archiving thoughts and intentions
Some plant seeds and tweet
Self-serving deeds of enmity

Unlike birds who rest in cozy nests
They spin out of control
By Jove, they take aim
Watch as truth flees

Falling flat on face, they descend
Into the depths of a black hole
Opiate for perversity's greed
What they want, they take

contemplation

he turned around, he looked back
yet difficult to believe
so many dreams had gone by
at least decades of them
none of them survived
which way did they turn
never to say again
what had been left unsaid
when last time, lost
promises wilted as the drought
of emotions, buried at sea
discontented waves of dreams
measured in thoughts
of implausibility, nothing else to do
no one here or there
the years of fears
nor the sea of possibility

he turned around, he looked back
nothing could he do, no one survived
so why waves he a flag so faithfully
now, seeing a shriveled ship of hope
on the horizon, he thinks it a ghost
sadly, it sinks in desperation
the mirage and he both wizened

what is there now to say
what is there now to do
there is no one here or there
there is nothing he can do
except to bathe in the sea of reality
and begin life anew

Jackie Davis Allen

Chasing Sleep

When night comes
And sleep does not
And the clock tick-tocks
The one standing tall, in the hall

Like a mysterious sentry
My mind plays games with each
And every sound that comes
As the house begins its cool-down

I chase the white sheep, the black ones, too
And wonder what more
Than counting them
Might I do

To catch a good night's sleep
And so, I pray as I may
As I must, close my eyes and
Think to resign my sleep to trust

Time for Prayer

Tick tock, tick tock.

The hours have slowly gone by, seems an eternity, though it has been less than half a day, since James left to fetch the doctor. All the while, our little son tosses and turns, coughing and hacking, feverish and out of his head.

    James and the doctor now move toward the mantle, wooden-like, like marionettes without strings. They knock their feet against the grate. Clumps of ice fall into melting puddles. The two men sink down on the tall, hand-carved, black walnut bench and begin to remove their boots. And, massage their benumbed feet.

Tick tock, tick tock.

The hands on the clock are frozen in place, even as my heart races with worry. In the next room, while the men thaw out their bodies, our little son continues to gasp for breath. I fear he is on the verge of death. Scarcely can I keep from screaming: "Will you hurry!"

    But as patient, I must be perceived, for it is the doctor who has the skill in his hands to save Tommy. I am praying he can revive our little son, who lies listless behind the door. Silent, except, for his rattling breath.

Tick tock, tick tock.

It seems ten years have passed since they arrived, though less than ten minutes by the grandfather-clock, whose hands have no skill except to tell the hour. Now, it is in God's hands. His and the doctor's.

    The doctor adjusts his glasses, now dried from the steaming fog, and prepares to enter the room where our son lies waiting. My hands and James' hands are folded in prayer. On bended knee, we pray our son's life be spared, and again, made whole. *We entrust him to You, our Heavenly Father, the Great Physician.*

Scratchy breath, coughing, hacking, and now, the doctor calls out, "Have you any onions?"

No time to ask any questions. So, I say, "Yes, we do."

"Fry them up in some grease, and hurry, bring them to me in a towel."

Pleased to be enlisted to help, James peels and cries. I slice and dice. And cry, too. We are happy to have an excuse to explain away our fears. And frying them in the hot skillet with bacon fat, we deliver the poultice to the doctor in an iron skillet to retain the heat.

Tick tock, tick tock.

The doctor accepts the onion poultice and lays them on our dear son's chest. It seems, he is breathing better already. "He will live, if he makes it through the night. We must keep up the application." As he speaks, he selects a bottle from his bag and pours out a spoonful of brandy. Lifting up our little son's head, he pours the liquid down his throat.

"Every three or four hours, a teaspoon, no more, no less. Hopefully, by breakfast, we will know for sure if we have been successful. The rest is in God's hands."

Exhausted, the three of us alternate praying, napping and checking on Tommy.

Tick tock, tick tock.

As day breaks, a sweet voice rings out.

"Mommy? Daddy? Where are you? I am hungry!"

Here I Am

Looking through memory's window pane
I see sheer curtains, they, freshly
Unpinned from stretcher-frames

My little house sits beside the road, at the same
Time, it is adjacent to the foot of the mountain
And, at the level of the painted metal rooftop
The ping-ping of rain sings

A regiment of colorful iris stand
At attention, blades sharpened
Awaiting review

Surrounded by a bannister, the front porch
Serves as a guard, with arms to confine feet
Wanderings, those sorely tempted to stray
Down danger's narrow roadway

Coal trucks speed, as if on a racetrack
Their loads as dark and heavy
As the men are true

Two front doors lead into my house
Silent, beneath the bead board-ceiling, painted
Blue, each awaiting friend or foe; everyone
Knows the doors are never locked

In the corner of my room, near the window
Next to twin Jenny Lind-beds
A mouse-hole awaits

And the mouse waits for a piece of cheese
He often previews the scene, surreptitiously
Checking to see if the coast is clear
Small and insignificant, he holds life dear

Jackie Davis Allen

On the window-sill sits Snowshoes
A Maine Coon-cat, her eyes are marked
Strikingly dark, like mascara

Hair straight and curly; her prim demeanor
Compares with that of a ballerina
Minus the extra legs. And her mitten paws
Of course, that is how she became so named

A mirror painted in reverse, hangs on the far wall
Its cabbage-roses rest on a faded paper trellis

In muted shades of green, decades ago
The sun had its way, or so I have been told
The patchwork quilt and the heirloom-spread
Treasures covering the antique beds

On the pine board-floor
Painted mustard yellow, a border
Stained dark walnut in color

Worthy of a princely sum, a Persian rug
In royal purple's splendor, reclines
Gifted by a favorite aunt; friends believe
Erroneously, that we are wealthy, rich

The truth
Financially
Is that we are not

No Illusions . . . through the looking glass

A New Day Is Here

A long time ago
Back in the mountains of Appalachia
A little school girl, passionately, invested
Time and effort printing
Handing out flyers
Hoping, praying, her candidate might win

Alas! Her heart dropped, as over the radio
She heard another had won the coveted prize

Back in class
She was ashamed to show her face
The competitor and her classmates
Celebrated, gloated, cheered
While she beseeched God
The winner be given grace and insight

Despite her sorrow and fears, she spent time
In prayer, asking Him to make things right

She continued on
Just as she had before the fall
But when she came of age, she cast
Her first vote for her parents' choice
Wiser, she now makes up her own mind
Invites sore losers to grow up

Jackie Davis Allen

Consideration

The definitive, descriptive definition
Of my concept of consciousness
Is found in the face of responsibility.
It mimics the mirror that others see.

A pleading voice at my door
Entreats, encourages and entices me
To seize the best of the moment
And to dive into opportunity's possibility.

With potential's emancipation, creativity's
Chains are once again loosened
For exploration and for exploitation.
Lo! I have become a consideration.

Dare I hesitate a moment to ponder,
To inquire at what cost, at what price
Success arrives? And, if the gift given,
Now uncovered, is good for mankind?

Ode to Never-More

Hear now this dark and twisted tale
Know thee, verily well, the truth behind
Anger's chilling sorrow and woe

I caught a furtive glance inside her soul
Sensed how twisted was her house of mind
And how unhinged was its door to peace

As a reluctant listener but an invited guest
She told me her innermost secrets
They far too terrible to recount

No bonfire could have compared
To the face of anger's hurt, or her grief
Nor could any have imagined the tale she told

Her haunted-eyes were wide, dark and filled
With angst of remembrance, she, traveling
As an apparition, a nightmare's account of pain

The pain of capture and the taking of her innocence
Alas! No comfort did she own. Her voice silenced
By revenge's resulting consequence

So dastardly were the acts, deeds inflicted
My heart cried. Yet, had I openly wept from fear
Or compassion, she may have wavered in the telling

Too long had she borne her cross alone
She, but a child, even now. Sympathetic
Shocked by what I heard, I was appalled

Horrified, and at a loss for words
How terrifying it was. The least I could do
Was to lend her my time, my listening ear

Jackie Davis Allen

Pity, sympathy filled my heart; the poor creature
But a skeleton of her once virginal youth, yet
She became calm, moving toward a catharsis

It was if a century passed while she unpeeled
The facade that mirrored who she had become
She, unburdening shame's tainted secrets

She seemed younger, and I, humbled, more
Compassionate. I thought about the ghosts
That deprived her of rest, sleep and peace

It was no wonder she had morphed into bitterness
Devoid of trust. Yet, how was it that she had come
To place her confidence in me?

Without thinking, I cradled her in my arms
And as if on wings' flight and, yes, of compassion
I carried her out to the mountain spring

We knelt down into its cleansing waters
Where we prayed, her tumultuous past
And its flood of memories be no more

God Only Knows

I wrote a poetic poem one auspicious day
Wrote everything down, wrote what I had to say
Yet, to my Muse I must give credit, and repay
It was she who kept me from going astray

Crafting the composition, God, my Muse and I
We knew full well that day what it meant to cry
The gift of confidence, they gave a full supply
Encouraging words, the poem, with which to apply

So desperately-needed, more than mere money
For the rent, at last, empowered, I did relent
My third version of the verse to the editor
To be sent; I was most pleased with what that meant

When later asked, my creation to represent
To respond to the poem's purpose, intent
I thought, Oh, God, I once knew what it meant
Now I am in a most terrible predicament

I requested, received, more time to reply
My Muse was silent, the days, weeks went by
Leaving me to wonder, could memory supply
The who, the what, the how, or the why

In desperation, I wrote in my reply: God only knows
Pleased that the editor, my poem, he did not deny
He sent me a check, barely enough for me to get by
And in his note to my reply, he wrote

I accepted Browning's explanation, thereby
I accept yours, on this auspicious day in July

Jackie Davis Allen

clueless

heartless, the cold shrieking winds
obsessively streak and morosely howl
they are a foretelling of winter's dividend

blossoming beneath the azure-blue
the day's white-hot sunbeam-eye cracks
through my hazy perspective

the taste of the deep sea's icy breeze
and my lingering malaise are no comfort
they befriend my heart, wear my chemise

and, pounding the beach of sanity
I continue to search for a way to reconcile
the immeasurable grief of death's inhumanity

the wind, swept past of our history, sifts down
resolutely, surely, to where no voices reach
to where, two days ago, my lover drowned

apprehensive of clues, I still pace the shore
as he slumbers beneath, in his watery grave
I weep, call his name; woefully, he is no more

pounding the beach of sanity, I strive
to find a reason for his too soon-demise
I am perplexed as to how I am to survive

Always

Yesterday is no more
It is neither dependent upon
Whether I remember it or not

Today is what I have got
So, what am I to make
Of its golden treasure

Both the good and the bad
The beautiful and less so
Have come, invited or not

In this moment, as I sit here
I am thinking about the blessings
Most bountiful, that I have received

For the gift of life, for second
Chances, for opportunities
To make for others, a smile

Jackie Davis Allen

The Thread Unraveled

O brilliant mystery, reigning down
I marvel at your resplendence
Reflected by your dazzling crown

Unable am I, for my crime to offer defense
Indicted, obediently and attentively low
I bow before your autonomous renown

The tarnished trumpets sound so loud
With immediacy, with immense intent
Over all the surrounding villages, towns

And I, suffering from lack of counsel
Have nowhere to turn, to fathom how it is
You can smile beneath your jeweled crown

Once, in my love, you nearly drowned
We were one, with no claim of pretense
And, as my privilege is revoked, I am bound

To condescend, to reveal our affair: your offense
And so, I ask, why do you disavow the babe
Meek and mild, our very own love-child

The Matchmaking Snafu

Momma enlisted one of her sisters to stay with me while they went out of town to attend a funeral. I am not sure why they left me at home. I have forgotten which of her many sisters volunteered to babysit me. For this tale, I will say it was aunt Kathy, young, single, and a good match for my pastor. She was pretty. And, if I had told her about my plan, she would not have agreed.

    Somehow, she and the Pastor had to get together and I had figured out a way to make that happen. Pastor was a bachelor. He preached at both the church down the road and the one up the road. My sisters and I attended both Sunday School and church services at one or the other places. He was a frequent guest, coming as invited dinner guest, or simply dropping in unexpectedly.

    It is my belief that the idea to play matchmaker with Pastor and my aunt was all mine. One of my sisters, until recently, was a firm "in control"-person and a "dispenser of justice". She was not there and knew nothing of what was to transpire, or else she would have spilled the secret. And, it was a secret, right up to the end.

    Inviting Pastor was no problem, even though I do not recall whether or not I lied and said something like, "Momma and Poppa would like you to come to dinner." Or, perhaps I simply deceived him by saying, "We want you to come to dinner." In any case, he accepted, not having any reason to decline.

    Now, aunt Kathy, she had no knowledge of what I was up to. Cooking dinner was the norm and other than the vase of flowers on the table there was nothing to arouse suspicion, that is, until Pastor showed up. For dinner we had, or rather, we prepared corn-bread, made in Momma's often-used iron skillet. Along with pinto beans, our daily staple, and sour kraut, we also had sliced cucumbers and tomatoes from the garden. I did not tell aunt Kathy that we were expecting a dinner-guest, although she had wondered about the flowers.

She knew me quite well, remembering, I am sure, earlier in the summer when her sister Amelia and I completely rearranged Grandma's kitchen. Everything, except the cookstove and the kitchen-sink.

    We moved the free-standing kitchen cabinet and switched it with the refrigerator. We rearranged everything in the cabinets and in the refrigerator. We moved the table and chairs to a different orientation. We took down the pictures and hung them back up where we thought they looked best. We even mopped and waxed the linoleum floor until it was not safe to walk on. Not only did it shine and glimmer like ice on a skating rink, it was just as slippery. Grandma was not at all pleased with me or with her daughter. After all that hard work, we had to put everything back where it belonged. So much for our interior design and decorating attempts.

    Pastor knocked on the door. Once inside, he saw the table, set with flowers, the mis-matched water glasses and two plates. Immediately, he knew something was wrong.

"Where are your parents?"

Aunt Kathy also knew something was wrong. She and I were not going to be the ones sitting down to dinner. Her face reddened. In embarrassment, she fled to the back room. Pastor stammered. The red flush, rising up from his neck and slowly spreading all over his face.

"I think there has been some mistake. I have to leave."

I do not remember what Momma and Poppa said when they found out what happened. Perhaps, they never knew? Would Pastor have told my parents? Would aunt Kathy have told my mother or father? I do not know if they would have wanted to bring the subject up, as the embarrassment would have been considerable. Had my eldest sister been present, I am sure she would have told my parents, she, who would have never indulged in such subterfuge.

∙ ∙ ∙
175

No Illusions . . . through the looking glass

A little more than a year later, and after having failed in my attempt as an interior decorator and as a matchmaker, I became a thief. Maybe you heard about Sally and me stealing some Sunday School materials? Pastor, turned amateur sleuth, discovered that materials were missing from the church. And, that I was the thief.

Jackie Davis Allen

Milking Time

The roosters and the chickens scattered over the naked and dusty yard. I skipped up the steps to the nearly century-old whitewashed and hand-hewn board and batten house. Its patina now matched the color of the boxcars and their coal black load, chugging along down the railroad tracks.

Whoo a Whoo! Whoo a Whoo! The engineer tooted his whistle, and the steam-powered locomotive snaked around the mountain, leading a procession of boxcars loaded with coal, spewing out plumes of smoke and black cinders that left their imprint upon the still-damp wash hanging on the clothes line in the front yard.

"Chick, chick, here chick, chick, chick." The chickens came a' running as Lizzie, a spinster by calling, sat out on the porch with me. Her apron held several dried ears of corn. She shelled one and tossed the corn to the two-legged critters, they, rushing as in a competition to see who would win the prize.

"Cock- a-doodle-do!" The head of the harem crowed. With white breast puffed out, he and his concubine hens dispersed. They, letting their master have his way with the corn, just as he had his way with them. Red Top had no other competitor living nearer than two miles away.

Lizzie stood up. She dusted off her apron, adjusted her glasses, and stepped down the rickety steps. Of necessity, she held onto the handrail that once had seen better days. The two of us went around the back of the house in search of Patsy, the cow. She was mooing, announcing it was time to relieve her of her milk.

Lizzie crossed the footbridge, and the two of us clambered up the hill. Lizzie carried a peeled bark-stick for a cane. Rising to meet the ridge, we waited to cross over the railroad tracks to where Patsy waited, as it seemed she did most days. Ginger, running as if to catch up with us. Whoo . . . whoo . . . a whoo . . . The train faded from view as it went around the bend. "I declare, Patsy. You are the most stubborn of cows."

And Patsy, nodding her head ever so slightly, just enough to cause the bell around her neck to clang, swished her tail to the side. And, slapping a fly or two, she perked up when she heard Ginger barking. They have a long history, one in the herding and the other in the responding.

The wind was blowing, and the butterflies were flitting here and there. Down along the hillside, honeysuckle was growing, its orangey and spicy blossoms were an invitation to the bees. Lizzie maneuvered down the hill, me following her, her brogans digging in deep. Aided by her walking-stick, she came to a rest at the foot of the hill. Patsy, urged on by Ginger's encouragement. And, stopping by the creek, Patsy drank slowly, and, as was Ginger's nature, she barked and barked as if to say, we have got to be going along.

Lizzie and I arrived back at the house a bit after Ginger and Patsy did. Flitting from tree to tree, the birds began to sing their songs. One blue bird, sitting on the barbed wire-fence, dove toward Lizzie's head with a ferociousness that belied that little blue bomber's size. She attacked Lizzie in an attempt to protect her young, even as she chattered. Lizzie, regaining her composure, smoothed her graying hair as I tagged along behind her. Patsy and Ginger rehearsed their introductions once again.

I sat down next to Lizzie. She, rhythmically, squeezing on Patsy's teats. Contented, relived, Patsy consented, and the pail began to fill.

Jackie Davis Allen

Of Life and Loss

In autumn of days, golden hues embrace
The meaning of life, its loves, its losses
Thankful for the treasures, of nature's gifts

As nature's face slows the pace, it merges
Memories, blurs, forgives, sad for the reason
Why a life, long-lived, falters at the end

Waiting on the shore, there remains rare
Remnant of a shell, bruised icy-white
Cold, old, with failing frosty breath, asleep

Alas! Night falls. So too the first snowfall, and
As sorrow blankets the night, it moans, wails
Soon, perhaps, it will yield and take flight

Chimera

Click-clack, click-clack
I am walking down the street

And it is midnight
Such a vaporous night
Even though the lamplights are burning

My heart is racing, for I think
Someone's following me

Yet, I am unable to hasten
Or to quicken my pace
Someone IS following me

Click-clack, click-clack, click-clack
Now, I'm running down the street

In the misty fog
Beneath the lamplights
Shadows are dancing with the moon

Bare branches bend and wave
The wind rustles, pops and crackles

Echoing the drumbeats is my heart
A monster, I do believe
Is following me

Click-clack, click-clack, click-clack
Click-clack, click-clack, click-clack

Jackie Davis Allen

The musical refrain, relentlessly
Counts the time, measures each step
Crystal bells begin to clang

Determined to revise
This overture and, attempting

To calm my fears
I rub my eyes, roll up my sleeves
And attempt to save my sanity

Click-clack, click-clack, click-clack
I throw open the loosened shutters

And let in the light of the morning
Filled with the fresh air of the day
The free weights of the night's terror

Are no longer holding me hostage

Sunrise

Sunrise, hot, impressed
Awakening to blue skies
A breezy morning
Walking on the beach
Strolling white sands

Alone with my thoughts
Feet wave-washed-wet
Sharp shadowy reflections
In my hand, sea glass-smoothed
Resurrection of past life

Peace and earth's gifts
The azure-blue sky, sun-kissed
Surprised, I am not
To see three sea gulls
Hungrily, following me

Jackie Davis Allen

Adjustments

Never was she a model
For the world of fashion

And yet, throughout the years
And despite her figure, its shape
She had a tendency to follow the trends

She cycled up and down
And all around, trying to find

The blueprint, the formula
If you will, to approximate
The classics in design

Which she, habitually, wears
She dresses only in that

Which approximates the pattern
Of her intention, a phenomenon
That characterizes

The varying traits of her behavior
And her attitude

interlude

sing to me
gentle poet
soothe
my aching heart
lift my somber spirits high
for ominous
and darkening skies
and wildest winds
rushing by
would, as I, on sorrow's bed lie
awaken
despairing visions
which would seek
to hide
from me
the morrow

Jackie Davis Allen

farewell

icy cold, the winds collect, gather
shivering streaks of winter collide
they, with diamond bright sunbeams
crackling through the harrowing haze
and, solemnly and heavily cloaked
while I survey the cliffs
through the mysterious mist
as the wind strewn-past
sifts resolutely down

on time's immortal shore
they glide by on passionate waves
and grieving, bleeding hearts
pound the beach of sanity
are searching for ways to reconcile
the searing pain of sorrow, insufferable
incessant tears continue to fall down
and as the salty waters crash
against the relentless ocean-tides

protesting the demise
of this brave one, militant taps
and mournful wails
sail out on brass notes
drifting into the deepest darkest sea
sorrow wraps her arms around me
and I remain inconsolable
the golden orb, sliding down
to meet its watery grave

Beyond Definition

Stardust fills the throbbing sky
And love trips over the moonbeams
While a chorus of angels sing for joy

The night is a musical composition

Venus smiles over her celestial realm
Wonderment invokes wanton-wistfulness
Sensuality breathes fragrance of romance

The flame of man's passion, ignited

Stars relenting, reflect their light
A taste of passion expands possibilities
A universe of caressed emotions gives birth

And, my beloved and I indulge in love's intimacy

Asteroids trip over a host of galaxies
Desire ignites and awakens ecstasy
A supernova explodes its luminosity

And our love soars ever heavenward

Jackie Davis Allen

Aching

The garden's silence breathes in the dawning
A whisper, perchance of winter calling
Startles morning's solitude

Face, warmly lit. Smile, perhaps, tinted pink
The early morn', when with the golden orb
Waves its prescient warning

A treasure, months and months of memories
Dark melancholy's wings. They are shadowing
My sanity. I am weeping

Beneath a canopy of anxiety
I am falling down, losing hope, searching
My pain, increasing. The name of needing

Painted another way, I am secreting
Arrangement of tears and fears
And, for him, I am still waiting

Poetic Elixir

Returning home, I sat, so alone
Spinning my half-empty glass
Of memory on the table
Certain, it would quite knock me out
So heady was the pleasure
Of finding you among the aisles
Of the reigning poetry books

You were wearing a crown of smiles
Intently tipping your head back up
Into the aching clouds
I tore off your clear coat of immunity
Yawned and devoured the words
Above the enticing title
Now, I flash back to the hall

Of mirrors when hormonal
Buds of youth filled the garden
With eye-candy, where with
Pirouetting feet, not yours though
Left me wilting, a flower, faded
Twining up from the perfumed garden-wall
Now, I idly pick up myself and inhale

The crystal truth. I am inebriated, staggering
To return to the aisle for more of your elixir
You have kept yourself so close-by
While I have consumed decades of poetic stanzas
Yet, when I pick up your newest composition
And peruse you through the window of time
I am exhilarated, overcome by your eloquence

Jackie Davis Allen

Are You Still There?

Where are you?
Are you still my faithful friend?
Once a comfort in time of need,
I long for your presence.

Do not pretend that I do not exist.
O come!
I beg, plead, please come
With words of encouragement.

O please, come to my rescue!

Come, support
My flailing determination!
Revive me for I long
To produce works, creative.

Come, o my muse,
O please, come to me!
Rescue me!
Come, be my friend again!

No Illusions . . . through the looking glass

Some Dreams Do Come True

Snuggled up
Like buns in the oven
Three-month-old twins
Asleep in a bassinet
Surrounded by music, a lullaby
Crooning a soothing tune

On the pink papered-walls
A castle; nearby, a fairy princess
A prince and a frog
They prance merrily
On the mossy green landscape
It is as if they are actually dancing

Happy as the sunshine
Are the fluttering fringes
Decorating the sides, the tops
Of the yellow, pink and white curtains
Imprinted, with fancy little bows
The babies, were they asleep?

The mother peeks into the room
Finds them smiling, cooing
Satisfied they are happy
Contented with each other
She returns to her chores
Singing, a smile on her face

Jackie Davis Allen

No Need for Dialogue

Superimposed
Against the giddy scenario
The evening is a surrealistic dream
Attired in tuxedo and bow tie
With the pleated-front, white shirt

He holds her snugly
Encircling her waist like a cummerbund
And, beneath the watchful eyes
Of the celestial moon and stars
He and his adoring partner dance as one

Transfixed by intimacy's possibility
Their music mutes the band
And, while searching, hungering pairs
Of lips give and receive kisses
There is no need for dialogue

Dilated, fixated, their eyes
Focused, solely, intently upon
Each other; breathing heavily
It is as if they are in a champagne-bubble
Swallowed up by passion's desire

Charting the Course

She allowed her pen and pad
Instruments of her voice
To continue as they led from design
Even behind the lines

She collected expectant pauses, phrases
Some of joy, some of sadness
That flashed on the screen
Of her fertile mind

Dusting off the decades
Of her prolific poetry
She saw that some seeds she had sown
Had bloomed, some before their time

With persistence's fragrance
The inked sheets beckoned
Thirsty crowds, and with excitement
Celebrated the moment

With wisdom, she continued extracting
From her gifts and talents
Words of healing balm, and prayed
God might grant her a little more time

Jackie Davis Allen

Like India-Ink

From presumption
To presentation
His salient pen foretold
Illusion's sordid theme
Yet, that, he denied

In moments of delusion
Ego all but seduced him

Behind the door, painted
In shades of garish neon-red
The mawkish blue-green walls
Stood as silent witnesses
Whispered contempt

Aghast at the scattered pages
Lying on his unmade bed

Had he captured all
The prolific and pregnant pauses
Had he portrayed the best
Of mystery's illusion
Had he . . .

Had he, with phrases poignant
Illustrated motivation's cause

From his greed, his need
Passion's personification
Spilled out like an ancient river
It bled like India-Ink, in honor
Of all those who had served

the ocean

frothy, foaming sea
swirling, unfurling life
glistening sun-rays

silently, I lie
beneath the salty waters' solo
high tides crashing, splashing over me

at the mercy of the moon
I am submerged
hear the sea gulls roar

cymbal-like applause
reaches a roaring crescendo
then becomes as quite as can be

sedated, the salty waters croon
and I, the sandy beach
emerge once more

skimming surface, mirror-like
the ocean, the sea is God's gift
to all of humanity

indite

encircling the passage
strings of perils
rattle the repose of life

in the blue of showers
buds flower
day and night

hidden in the house of mind
behind private doors
keyed by pen

and viewed as paper trails
stains of blood-orange
sting sweet her life

bleed they, her brow
tainted by turmoil
evidenced by ringing bells

firestorm, lighting candles
of principle
haunt spirits

paths bud, blossom
then guide as she begins to indite
with the bones

A Feather in Her Hat?

Residing
Beneath celestial mystery
Deep within the recesses
Of her mind, there exists
An intriguing intellect
Imaginatively conspiring

To construct creations
Of poetical nonsense
Selectively
Subversively
She variously
Selects odd themes

The gems from which
She derives verses, lines
After which, if successful
She defines the struggle
Whether or not
It merits the eye of approval

Jackie Davis Allen

Videos, Redactions and Lies

Cool, the morning breeze
And there, high above, from a mountain-waterfall,
Splash icy cold, crystal overflowing
There, where thirst's promise is satisfied
A nation longs for that which will protect it
And make of its creativity a beautiful song
Dark is the recess, in contemplation
Where the heart beats, where no one can see
Fear's ravenous consumption
Where hope is held hostage by tourniquet's silence
There, in a sliver of light, one dares attempt a plan
Of escape, despite woeful wounds of infection
Hot sears the sun's heat, dazzling rays
Yet, her face, she hides as she hesitates
Gliding in slow motion her upward path
High across the sky. A visitor, reluctant.
We are inclined to say, her face is revealed
Only at the mid-mark of each and every day
Eyes open slowly; the wheels
Of decision's conflict call for a change
In leadership; the enemy spouts alarm
Chants, taunts with terror's destruction.
Can the kaleidoscope of truth coexist with discernment
When common sense and reason have gone awry?
Multicolored are the facets
Of evil's danger; insidious, his face
As are his reflections, refractions, deceptions
Alas! Those who breathe lies
Violate a people's sense of safety
They, who hide
Behind videos, redactions, and lies

Intentions

He waded through the strained
And stained pages of time
Disenchanted by anonymity
Disregarding his gifts
Talents and ability

He thought of navigating by the stars
Whose light disbursed hope
And mystery against the landscape
Of his mind, yet, decided to ignore
The possibilities

Led to the rivers of truth
By some strange force, though troubled
By the voices trashing around inside his head
He envisioned the sleep of the deep
And sank beneath the swirling surf

Flailing, he floundered, then heard he
A voice reaching out to him
Rise up, use your gifts
Time is of the essence
Swim, or else, today, you'll drown

A pathetic man, one less than
And thus, excluded from history
Swim, or else you and your gifts suffer
Evisceration in pity's waters, the poverty-pool
Of everlasting and intentional misery

Jackie Davis Allen

First Edition

A treasure, I found, at such a fair price
For a book, its author unknown to me
And as a Christmas present, it I happily sent
To let my friend know I was thinking of him

If the truth be known, the wrapping paper
The postage, too, were greater than the paltry
Amount that I withdrew from my account
To procure for him the generosity of my intent

Impossible was it for him to know the little
I spent, the book serendipitously discovered
In a charity shop; one, as if never read nor opened
So, promptly to the post office, I speedily went

In his handwritten thank you, he did share
How immensely, how intensely he had enjoyed it
That with his son, he thought to share, and to relent
The pleasure of his treasure, my Christmas present

The title of the book is one I have long forgotten
But not the thought of the pleasure it gave him
His son, too, naming his new puppy by the same
Name, given to a town: the one on the book jacket

Perusing the web, the internet, more recently, he
Sought to discover what other readers thought
Only to find that the cost of the book, the one
I bought, had increased by immeasurable percent

Hungry

Seven seagulls gathered, seeking relief
Hoping to find something tasty to eat

And large as sand dunes, the many mistakes
Of her youth threatened to overwhelm her
Invited by apprehension's sad wake

A child, holding his father's hand, offered
Crumbs of bread to an advancing seagull

As fire-stained days and weeping ways
Waged war, invaded, she hoped to bury them
In the well of the ocean's salty waves

Below the blue, above rocky cliffs
Standing by, silent in repose

Tides of concern washed four-score years
Over indecision, she wallowing
In pity, on sorrow's forever shore

A tear, a smile, then a seagull's cry
Encouragement, for giving life a try

Crashing cymbals, roaring sea, deafening
By degrees, yet in a moment, life changed
She thought she heard him calling her name

Jackie Davis Allen

First Grade: A Troubling Beginning

Momma parked the car alongside the road. We walked down the steps to the front of the school, turned right and followed the sidewalk to the back side of the school.

There we were, Momma and I, she carrying my little brother, and my younger sister tagging along, tugging at her skirt. My heart was thumping with fear, and my thoughts and breathing were racing, as we climbed up the steps. The heavy door groaned as Momma reached out, holding it open. The auditorium was the largest room I had ever seen. The back section, near the stairs we had just climbed, was filled with windows that rose above the steam-radiators, the windows reaching up to the ceiling. Yellowed pull-shades were askew, some raised, some lowered, but all available to darken the room when needed. The floor was dark and old, and oiled. It was slippery.

I closed my eyes, as if transported, and continued walking across the back of the auditorium. We turned left, and there before us, the corridor. It appeared dark and foreboding, much like a scary tunnel to my searching eyes. There were no windows in this darkened dungeon-like space, only two double doors at the end. And, there was a lady standing at the entrance to what was my first-grade room. My teacher. Momma encouraged me, saying, "Go on, now. You're a big girl. Just walk on down the hall and say good morning. Your teacher will show you where to put your things and you can pick out your very own desk." I begged Momma to come with me, to walk with me. Wise woman, she insisted I go on, alone.

"You can do it. And, I'll see you when you get home."

If that comment was supposed to be comforting, it was not. I was afraid, thinking about the end of the day, that, somehow, I would get on the wrong bus.

So, off I went. Consumed by doubt and insecurity. I did manage to say good morning to the tall lady. There was a row of desks, directly in front of the door. I selected the second one from the back of the room. A wide bank of windows, rising above the steam heat-radiators, was to my back. The teacher sat in front of the room. The wall, opposite my teacher's desk, held the students' cloakroom. Teacher had her own closet, at the far end of the students' cloakroom. It had a door that came with a lock and a key.

I already knew how to read and write; my mother's baby sister had taught me. Besides, I had an older sister. I would be able to do my own work but also that assigned to the third graders who sat on the opposite of the room. Even still, that left some free-time, boring time which I attempted to fill up by chatting with those children that sat behind me, in front of me, or on either side of me. Soon, I discovered that talking, whispering or looking like I was getting ready to do one or the other was prohibited. The punishment for getting into trouble, like I did, was categorized by many different levels of humiliation.

Believe me, the first two levels were awful, but the third-level, which I managed somehow to avoid, was even worse, but not as bad as the fourth-level. If caught, no excuses were allowed or accepted. Uh oh! I heard my name!

"March yourself right up to the chalkboard. Take a piece of chalk and, standing on your tiptoes, draw a circle on the board where your nose touches. Now, place your nose in the circle, with your hands behind your back. Maybe this will teach you to pay attention to the rules and not talk in my classroom."

It is unnatural to stand on one's tiptoes, one's nose pressed to the chalkboard and clasping one's hands together while held behind one's back. But, do you think Miss First Grade Teacher knew that? Or that she cared about what I thought? She did not. I tried not to cry. But I wanted to. Did I like my first-grade teacher? One guess, and you will have it right. I did not like her. Not one little bit. Neither on the first day of first grade, nor would I on the last day.

If ever a teacher had eyes in the back of her head, then my teacher did. I never TALKED. I whispered. Even though I was only six and a half years-old, I knew the difference between talking and whispering. But, do you think Miss First Grade Teacher cared? No. Anyway, I had my share of doing nose-chalkboard duty, but one day, Miss First Grade Teacher decided to elevate my punishment. She put a piece of tape on my mouth.

Well, I must say, that got my attention, especially when, as lunch time grew nearer, the time when we would all file out and walk down that long dark corridor, through the auditorium, down the steps and then into the lunch room. Miss First Grade Teacher told me that I had to wear the tape over my mouth and return to class with it still adhered. That meant, still stuck tight. Now, how in the world was I going to be able to eat? And, return to class with the tape still on?

I pulled off the tape, picked up a tray, slid it around on the rack before the display of luncheon offerings, selected a carton of milk, a bowl of soup and a baloney sandwich. I charged it, the entire ten cents that it cost. I moved on my way, finding an empty chair at a table with some of my classmates. After I ate, still feeling guilty and looking over my shoulder and all around to see if my teacher was spying on me, I placed the tape back on my mouth. Of course, it would not stay put. I held my hand over the tape, my mouth closed. Should she try to punish me further for having taken the tape off, I was determined I would tell her, I had to eat. And, besides, the tape is still on my mouth even if it is my hand that is holding it there. Fortunately, she did not say anything. I finally took the tape off and placed it on her desk. I did not dare put it in the trash can, wanting to be ready to replace it if needed.

Recess promised to give me a respite from all of the stress I had inside the classroom. Not only did my teacher not like me, I do not think she liked any of my classmates. She seemed to always be angry. Well, I was angry too. I was angry with her and I was angry with Dick and Jane, Sally and Spot of the pre-primer readers. I had never ever heard anyone talk like them. Nor had I ever seen a mother wearing high heels as she worked inside her house, like the one pictured in the book. And, the father? I did not know any father who wore a suit and a tie, never mind one who carried a briefcase. And, besides, what was a briefcase anyway? Flying kites, riding bicycles . . . what was the illustrator of the book trying to do?

The dreaded third-level of punishment involved being placed in the students' dark cloakroom. Inside, where there was a section that included the cool air-return. We, children, thought it was a ghost that moaned when, actually, it was the wind that went whoo, whoo, whoo. It scared the dickens out of us. I never, ever was placed in that dungeon but there were others who were. The crying that filled the classroom paralyzed us all into a state of shocked silence.

The fourth-level of punishment was the teacher's closet. Teacher frequently reminded us that she had the key and she would use it. I never graduated to the last two levels. Between Dick and Jane and Miss First Grade Teacher, first grade was not what I had hoped and dreamed it might be. But I survived and I made a secret promise to myself. At the end of the year, if I found out she was going to be my second-grade teacher, well, I just might not ever go back to school.

Jackie Davis Allen

Facing the Brick Wall

I cannot say how
Or from where within my mind
The poems, the ones who used

To come, came as they did, mostly
Fully-formed, I must say
Always, to my utter delight

Alas! The days march on
So too, the weeks, months
Alas! My pen has gone to sleep

To me it pays little attention
No poesies come to mind
Why has my gift gone into hiding

Most precious is the art, the creativity
Of composing, whether
By pen, or by tapping on keys

In the past, my work was a joyous pursuit
With ease, I penned poems, rhymes, odes
I had no need to pretend

So, why should I care what appears
Upon the pages? They, damp with fears
Should I not continue on, persisting?

Determined, I will nourish my pen's ink
And pray it shall continue to feed
Despite any and all resistance

Callie Mae's Story

If I had a known that Preacher Isaac was going to introduce me and tell everyone there that I was the one who wrote the poem, "A Glimpse of Truth", I might not have recited it.

I don't mind getting credit for good things I've done. It just didn't seem fitting that he was holding me up so that everyone, afterwards could come up and tell me what a good girl I was. And, what a good job I'd done. And, to brag on me so. I was embarrassed and hoped that I hadn't hurt aunt Susie and uncle Zack's feelings.

It didn't seem proper to upstage James' funeral. At least, that's the way it seemed to me. I really don't know, if in fact, I did upstage his funeral. It's just that's what I was thinking at the time I was reciting it. Looking back over it now, I'm a little embarrassed to have included the references to the ocean in my poem because I've never seen one except a picture in a book. But, if it bothered anyone, no one ever said anything to me.

Aunt Susie was sitting up front, just a few feet from the coffin. In a burst of great emotion, I guess, she suddenly realized that she'd never see her son again. At least not on this earth. So, she rushed up to his open coffin. As she leaned forward to give James a parting kiss, the lid almost fell on top of her head. Uncle Zack, ever alert, went up and quickly pushed the lid back. Then, he sat back down. He wasn't being callous; he did help her back to her seat.

James had been destined to be like his father, especially since the doctors said that aunt Susie wasn't likely to have any more children. That was another thing I couldn't get right in my head. How could the doctor know a thing like that? I was smart enough to know that no bird like a stork had ever been seen by any living person around Cow Pen Holler. Oops, maybe I should say, "Hollow?"

Unlike his wife, uncle Zack knew that if he stayed there, standing and staring down at his son's pale lifeless face, he wouldn't be able to hold back the tears. It wasn't seemly for a man to cry in public. So, he did what most all the other men I'd seen do, he held them back. He blew his nose noisily and occasionally, dabbed at his eyes. He kept on taking out and stuffing back his big red handkerchief into the back pocket of his bib coveralls. Only, we call them "overalls."

James' coffin was carved out of pine boards. Most folks stored an occasional spare coffin or extra pine boards in their attics, cellars or barns for just such a time as this. Uncle Zack made his son's coffin with the help of my Poppa. Really, it was just a wooden box, but it was a box made specially to bury someone in. Poppa let me come in and watch them. It was a deathly silence that surrounded the three of us, except for the sawing and hammering.

I had kept thinking about the cracks in the sides of the coffin where the boards didn't exactly fit. Nothing about the coffin could be called "snug as a bug in a rug." I worried about bugs crawling in once baby James was laid to rest in his pine box coffin. It was lined with white satin. Aunt Susie had gotten married in the dress it came from.

And, one day, my Grandma will be down there, lying in her coffin box. The same old thoughts going to go into my head again and get piled up in there like a cold snow bank. I'm just waiting the day when they thaw. But then, I wonder if I'll be able to find someone to help me sort them out when that happens.

Baby James and I were first cousins but we'd never get to know each other. I'd never babysit him like aunt Susie and uncle Zack promised. Being an only child, the only time I got to play with other children was when I was at school. When I complained, Momma said, "Look at it this way, Callie Mae. You have lots of time to develop yourself that other children don't have. Think about all the writing you do. You tell me when you'd have a chance to do all that if you were always out playing or gallivanting around?" I guess Momma had something there.

I was forgetting what he looked like. Wish I could have drawn a picture. No one in our family had a camera. And, if we had enough money to afford taking pictures, how would we know we'd have money to ransom it from the drug store once the negatives were printed out on paper? Something might come up and we'd need the money for something else. We had to be practical.

    I sat between Momma and Poppa. I guess you could say I fidgeted a lot, because I was looking first over across where Poppa sat, then over to Momma. She looked peaked. She didn't say anything. Matter of fact, she didn't seem like herself. She doesn't drink or smoke or anything like that, we are tee-totalers. But it did seem to me that she was a bit woozy, sort of like old man Charley after he's had a bit too much to drink.

    I tried hard not to look around to the back of the church. There were plenty of people in front of me, plenty of grown-ups, women crying, sobbing, and the men, sniffing, and blowing their noses. It was just too much to swallow, or as teacher would say, "too much to take in at one time". To take my mind off death, dying, crying, and all the sadness and sorrow, I occupied myself with checking out what everyone was wearing and how many people wearing spectacles were taking them off and dabbing their eyes.

    If I'd had a pencil and some paper, I could have started an interesting account for the book I'd write when I got older. There was plenty enough time to take lots of notes because Preacher Isaac certainly took his time with funerals. Probably, if he'd known what I was thinking, he would have said I was being sacrilegious. Whatever that means.

    It's a good thing that I'm used to storing up ideas and stories in my head because that really helped take my mind off the fact that James would not be around to see me graduate from seventh grade. Of course, he wouldn't have been very old then, but education was one of the things my Momma and aunt Susie set store by.

"You're going to graduate, even if I have to take in washing. And, you're going to go to high school if it kills me. I won't have you quitting before you finish high school and going off and getting married like too many young girls.

Mr. Blankenship is kin, and as such as he 'rules the roost' at the school, I'm sure he knows how to get you a scholarship. Sister Susie and I would never have been able to go off to college, even if I hadn't quit high school myself. I'm going to make sure you get settled into a good job. You know, you can be a secretary, a nurse, or even a teacher. You've just got to set your mind to it. "

What Momma should have known was that I had set my mind to it, as she said, but not in quite the way she was thinking. I was going to be a writer.

When Preacher Isaac prayed at funerals, he always called the one who had passed on, "our dearly departed brother" or "dearly departed sister". Actually, truth be known, he'd also called the older folks, "dearly departed mother, father, etc." Well, they weren't his kin, so, I don't know exactly why he had to insert himself into all those funerals. It wasn't as if he were related to any of them.

He preached so many funerals, maybe he felt like those that had passed on were his family? And that gave him an excuse to preach on and on, as if he had to reach the heart and soul of everyone, lest they died without having received the Holy Ghost? Momma and Poppa would most likely be just as surprised as Preacher Isaac, had they known what I was thinking.

Poppa once said aunt Vic was as ancient as the books he used in school. Why he thought to say that, I don't know. That aside, aunt Vic wisely pulled out her smelling salts and had them at the ready. She poured a little out of the vial onto a dainty embroidered handkerchief that she retrieved from her bosom. She handed it over to uncle Zack who placed it under aunt Susie's nose, for she was now sitting down. With a shudder and a bit of shaking, she steadied herself. Aunt Susie started to wail as loud as the church-bell when the fathers of some of her men-folk carried James' tiny coffin outdoors. The congregation filed down the center aisle. Each row on either side took turns, letting the others out, that is, after the family went out first.

The church might have been as old as Poppa's aunt Vic. I call her aunt Vic too. She wears a slate gray-colored hat with a black mesh like veil, spider web-like, to all church activities, even to rummage sales. The veil on her hat reminds me of the Little Church of the Brethren's stone-wall that's covered with ivy, moss and the ravages of time.

I don't know who it was I heard saying "ravages of time", but it sounds pretty good to me. I plan on using "ravages of time" in my book. I've not yet decided what the book will be about. I'm just gathering up material and will find a way to fit the pieces together when I've got enough. I hope I know when I've got enough.

Anyone who has ever heard Preacher Isaac preach a funeral can't say they don't know what they're in for. Hours and hours of holy roller-preaching. And, that's Sunday Service, weddings, funerals. All of it. I must say, I think I got blisters on my behind from having sat so long.

I don't think Preacher Isaac could possibly know that I'm going to write a story about the funeral and how he held us captive for all of the better part of three hours. I've already thought of a phrase I'll use in the story but got to figure out who will say it and how it should fit in. *Let's just be quick about it and get it done.*

It was such a relief to finally be able to get up and go outdoors, even if it meant trailing along behind the horse-drawn-carriage that would carry James to the graveyard. It seemed very rude that the preacher nailed the coffin lid shut right before our very eyes. No one else could bring themselves to do it, but it did have to be done.

We trudged along behind the carriage to the graveyard, the mourners singing, "Shall We Gather at the River". The elders of the church scattered straw around the opening in the ground where we stood. The preacher said a few words, perhaps more, but I don't recall what, just that there was such an eerie, echoing sound bouncing off one mountain against the other, magnifying the grief that we all felt. I shivered against the finality of death and the cold.

I've already decided to write my will. In it, I will state clearly that I don't want "Shall We Gather at the River" sung, and that, if Preacher Isaac has to be the one to preach my funeral, the entire service will last no more than half an hour. And, if I've written my book, I'll want someone to read certain selections. In that case, I'll make an exception and the service can last an hour. I'll mark the pages I want read. Of course, the preacher, whoever he is, can read some scripture, like from Psalms or maybe, just John 3:16. I want a party, so they can talk about something happy.

When they lowered my cousin, baby James, into the ground the sun was shining so. The sky was a wintery blue. There were no clouds, and on any other such day, one would have said it was, indeed, a lovely day. And, if truth be known, it was a lovely day. But grief colored it in such a way that I shall always hold the pain of that experience in my heart.

Still ringing are the words that Preacher Isaac said as we each tossed a small shovel of dirt overtop the gravesite: "James, our dearly departed little babe, lies here, his soul rests in the arms of Jesus, until the coming day when the dead in Christ shall rise." I haven't quite figured all this out, but I think it has something to do with getting a new body to match up with the soul. That's, when we get to heaven.

If I should die before my book is finished, I want one of my poems be read at my funeral. And, if I get married before I die, I'll have to change some of the words, but for now, here it is what it is. You'll note that I put the rosebush in the poem because it was blooming when baby James died. We had a snow-storm the next day. It covered up all the flowers that were on his grave. I never saw them myself, the flowers buried, that is, but the snow covered everything, about four inches-thick. Now, every time it snows, I pull out my poem and read it over and over. I've even got it memorized. Aunt Susie said she understood full well why it was so difficult for me to give names to my poetry. She helped me with the name of it. I've not yet had an assignment at school where I could turn my poem called "A Glimpse of

Truth" for a grade. But I've got it ready should Mr. Blankenship call for a poem about flowers, death and dying or the truth of things. Momma read it and said she thought it was way beyond my years.

"How could a child of your age be able to express in words what so many of us who are much older can't. Guess that's why God made some of his children writers and some not. You've got the gift, girl. Just keep on keeping on with your writing. You're going to make a name for yourself."

Then, Momma did something that she hadn't done before, ever. She went to her closet and took out her Sunday-meeting-hat and let me try it on. Oh, I'd been tempted to try it on many times before, and truth be known, I had succumbed to the temptation when she had been out in the garden working. I liked the veil that came down over my face, hiding the scar that hadn't smoothed out, next to my right ear. Most folks around here know that I almost died that day when Momma was doing the washing up on Cow Pen Holler. That's when I got burned.

Of course, since then, my hair has grown out and I don't need the hat to hide my scar anymore, my hair can do that just fine by itself. But, something in Momma's face told me that she had a lot of respect for me. And, since we're talking about the truth, I had to tell Momma something.

"Momma, I'm sorry, but right after the last skin-graft, I tried on your hat. You were out in the garden and I was hoping I could figure out how to hide the scar. I should have known you wouldn't let me wear your hat, but anyways, I tried on your hat. I'm sorry I didn't tell you when you came back from picking the green beans. I should have told you right then and there."

I was both surprised and pleased when Momma placed her hat on my head.

"Callie Mae, I knew you had been trying it on."

She tucked my hair behind my ears, and walked me over to the mirror that had been her grandmother's. The mirror looked like it was stained with smoke, but when I tried to rub it, it didn't come off.

"How did you know?"

"Well, sweetie pie, you never quite managed to put the lid back on the hat box so that the stripes lined up. And, there were a couple of times that you forgot to put my blue sweater back up on top of it. There was at least one time when you must have dropped my sweater when you were pulling down the hat box. You folded my sweater back up differently than I do. Never you mind. It's all right."

I began to cry. I was crying because my guilt had been relieved and because my Momma was the best Momma in the whole wide world.

No Illusions . . . through the looking glass

A Glimpse of Truth

Outside my window's view
There stands one
A winter rose blooming anew

Lying down below is baby James
Ever-loved, and ever so cold
Alone like sad rose
Beneath a drift of snow

The innocent gift, deprived of life
Hangs sweetly its head
Weeps with sorrow, bows its head
So sad is our loss

Ah, bleeds now, my heart
For words never said
Like the wind, it mourns, moans
Beating against the sand
Roaring across the sound

A glimpse of truth, my heart bled
When the news arrived
That you were no more, that you were dead
Ah, the winter rose, its scent, too, now lost

So great the pain, so too the cost
Like fog and mist, I am adrift
My dear James, you are sorely missed
My grief wails like a ship run aground

Callie Mae, 10 years old
Cow Pen Hollow

Jackie Davis Allen

Pleading Courage

For far too long, she stumbled
Afraid of the dark deep waters
Afraid of heights, having fallen
Into the crevices, where escape
Exacted too exorbitant a cost

Amongst life's choicest adventures
An offering of experiences
Both dark and sweet with wisps
Of spiraling steam, yet, her thirsty cup
Could not be filled enough

Like a hot Moroccan brew, stirred
With imagination of thick cream
Her thoughts glided, merged
With passion into the rays of the sun
Where below awaited a beach, pristine

Waves, capped with white frosting
Rode atop an array of various hues
Nearby sat a cozy little town
With pots of blossoms overflowing
With the fragrance of opportunity

Tracing paths of the azure-blue, she
With courage, beribboned with hope
Drifted into the surf, the water too deep
She protested, I am afraid I will sink
Inside a silent voice replied, just try

May I Awaken to a Better Day

As in a dream
Pedagogy raced unchecked. From sheep's hungry mores
Ethics howled, untamed, wore education's disguise
Then bleated and stomped his feet. Misguided

She trusted in the Heel of Achilles that had lost its foot

As in a dream
Didacticism abused, widened the stream while dubious
Essayists, called handmaidens, spouted propaganda's
Taint of fruit flies. Lies from the house of rhetoric's bed

Prognosticating arrogance's prose. She lived in her head

As in a dream
Taxes raised their heads, and from malevolent intent
A predator devoured a people's green backs, so too, their
Common sense. Unversed in truth, with script primed

Her alias robbed Peter, stole from all. Was it not a crime

As in a dream
By slight of hand, power grew and yes, Avarice corrupted
From greed's seed, design issued a stamp on cups of tea
The weak sheep tweaked . . . literally, with bared knuckles

Attacked some strays, caught too many in snares

As in a dream
The unseeing, clinging to the party-line, acquiesced
To her beckoning. And the unknowing, not to be denied
Placed fame's face on drawing cards. That is why she lost

Jackie Davis Allen

Crones, Weeds and an Exorcism

There are many weeds in my garden
their names of which I dare not speak.

They choke out the life of nature's beauty
and the dreams lying dormant at my feet.
Alas! The chokehold on my creativity,
is guarded by three old crones,
living inside of my head.

I have many opportunities
from which to choose, like painting and writing,
walking and dieting, which for some reason
I too often fail to attempt.
Although I know I have the resources,
time and talent.

I am hindered by lack
of motivation and inspiration
coming from the shrewish voices
inside of my head.
I am well aware that the gift of my talent
just might turn into weeds.
Unfortunately, it seems, lately, they have
cultivated as they have been
by the three old crones.

Undaunted, I summon up my courage
and donning my artist-smock,
I close the door to the
voices of the three old crones.
Gathering up my weapons,
the tools of my trade,

No Illusions . . . *through the looking glass*

I am determined to show the world of art
just what I think of those old crones.
I will paint until I collapse, if need be,
and once finished, I will submit
the piece to a juried show.

The names of the old crones
are Fear, Rejection and Failure.
Far too long, they have preyed
upon my confidence,
belittling my talent.

I know! I shall perform an exorcism!
Carefully, I begin to plan the event
which will take place
upon a gessoed canvas.

Fear will no longer be a part of me
for I will sever her ties
and make her to lie in a dark hole.
I will pile up all my regrets and cast them
to the side of the Mistress of Fear's grave.

Her wart-covered face, I paint bloody-red
and let it drizzle down over
her grayed gauntness.
And with my palate knife,
Her mouth and ears, I stuff
with stinkweed
and paint her eyes closed-shut.
I then lay her down
between the common St. John's-worth,
and the Scarlet Pimpernel,

Jackie Davis Allen

and with my knife
My trusty palate knife,
I vigorously attack
the old crone Rejection.

With long gnashing strokes,
I smear white paint on the ghastly face
of the old hag; I fill her degenerate
mouth with rotten eggs, and in her gnarled fingers,
I place a bouquet of poison ivy.
And partially cover her prostrate body
with Creeping Charlie.

Take that you, you old battle-axe!

So delighted am I with my painting,
I feel quite lightheaded.
After dispensing with the crones of
Fear and Rejection who used to live in my head,
I savor the moment.

And, now, holding my aching sides,
and laughing uproariously, I consider
how best to exorcise
Failure.

Standing back from my canvas, I see
the Mistress of Fear
lying in her grave, partially
covered with Creeping Charlie
and nearby, The Mistress of Rejection
lies between St. John's Worth
and the Scarlet Pimpernel.

No Illusions . . . *through the looking glass*

The painting will be complete
once the crone of Failure
has been put in her place.
Perhaps, I will paint her as a spectator
looking over her own shoulder,
aghast at what she sees.

Or, perhaps in anticipation
of her impending fatality
I'll have the miserable old crone peering
into a dark and empty hole,
her insignificant feet poised
on the edge of an ancient cliff.

Ah! Her foul mouth
I'll fill with bumble bees.
And on her head, I'll place a crown
of yellow flowers
delivered by the Black Medic.

The night of the Competition arrives,
and the acceptance of my painting comes
as no surprise to me,
for my confidence and talent
have resurfaced,
as a result of the demise
of the old hags who used to reside
inside of my head.
Having never exhibited
before, and unencumbered now
by the Three Old Crones,
I wander around the gallery.
Most anxious am I to check out the paintings

Jackie Davis Allen

of the other artists, and not a little curious
to hear what they might be saying
about my painting.

It is quite interesting
that many of the works of art on exhibit
feature weeds,
but none are as unusual as mine.

There are paintings
with lovely garden scenes,
which include a few unusual weeds
tucked in around garden gates.
And over there is a painting featuring
the very seedy and most promiscuous
Dandelion.

The awards are finally announced.

My painting of the *Three Old Crones*
wins "Best in Show"!

I hear my name, and proudly
step forward to claim my award,
and am asked to explain
how I came to paint this masterpiece.

Public speaking not being one
of my best attributes, I humbly
accept the microphone.

Ladies and gentlemen,
For far too long, the three old crones
Fear, Rejection and Failure
had taken up residence in my head.

No Illusions . . . *through the looking glass*

I likened them to weeds
and knowing weeds are stubborn
with insatiable roots,
I figured the best way
to rid myself of the old crones
was to exorcise them with
my trusty palate-knife.

The crowd roars their approval:
Bravo! Bravo! Bravo!

After I pocket the cash-award
for "Best in Show",
I cautiously walk along
the darkened streets toward my apartment,
wondering, if there are any relatives
of the three old crones
lurking in the shadows
waiting to take their revenge . . .

Jackie Davis Allen

Full Circle

If, by magic or otherwise
You could have come
Along with me, during my growing up-years
What might you have thought of me?

I crowned my head
With self-anointment's privilege
Winging my way in, around and over those
Whose stature and wisdom were far above my own

If, by mistakes made
One gains wisdom
Why did I not realize that they
Older than I, had more wisdom?

Punishment, mine, came in many forms
Confiscation of my library card
The deprivation of literature, most painful
I thought, I would starve

If, wisdom comes by education's way
How might one say, that from
Mistakes made, lessons learned
I have found my niche

And now, as an adult, when I reflect
Upon those adolescent days
I think it could not have happened
Any other way

rain-dance, rain-song

have you
felt the breath
of the wind
kiss your wings
with its sweet music
rising up
swirling every which way
the wind
inviting your feet
to leap joyously
into the puddles
from last night's rain?
and, in so doing
did your thoughts
turn away
from pain and angst
and with thanksgiving
you, once more
began to sing?

well done

crying spirits
so slight, so little
yet, deserving significance
offer too little appeal
to the preoccupied

often seen as without merit
soiled, wretched and abandoned
living in the well of despair
in the dark hiding-shame
their winsome faces

without power, minus names
their cries silenced by blame
against the echoing masses
scrambling up the ladders
toward excellence

the humble ones, seeking
a way to climb out of the muck
and mire of poverty, aspire
to ascend into the halls of education
seeking the light of day's work

and at the end of the day, they long
to rest satisfied with sufficient
enumeration for a job
well done, giving thanks
for opportunity's wondrous gift

Once Again

The year is just beginning
The cold and snow, falling down
A fire, I must light
That I might warm
To the idea
Of making peace
With the dark side
O Muse of the past
Fade thee the days
Of my angst
When with my pen
I find, not idle, in my hand
But rather a willing accomplice
To cooperate with ease
With the thoughts lying dormant
In my head
And that, with considerable
Reverence, with your assistance
I might transform them
Into words of poesy

Jackie Davis Allen

Tongue-in-Cheek

My dear Gramps, I am your grandson.
I look like you, and Momma says,
I act like you, talk like you, walk like you.

I am only a lad of twenty and two, and am
dreadfully sorry that I have never known you.

I am your grandson, dearest Grand-Mum.
Poppa says I'm generous, respectful, and kind,
That you would have been proud of me.

My dearest Grand-Mum, I'm twenty and two
And I am so sorry that I never got to know you.

Dearest love, I am your most ardent admirer.
I neither look like you nor think as you do.
I am my own person. I am undeniably me.

I am twenty and two, I am in love with you.
There's much about me that you do not know.

I am your husband, my love; my darling wife.
I am generous and respectful to a fault.
But, if ever I should be cross or unkind

May you always remember when first we wed.
You were but a teen, and I only twenty and two.

The Dream

Twisted, gnarled branches
Silhouetted against the darkening sky
Blackbirds flocking, squawking
Fleeing the sorrowful
Wind swept-landscape
Of a child's sigh
Torrential rains
Striking, frightening, wounding
Ravens hiding
Cawing, cawing, crying
Over the anticipated desire
For life's symphony
Dayspring, summer flowers
Sprouting, emerging
Bluebirds chirping, singing
Returning, renewing
Nature, and desiring
Something more
Hot, bright scalding light
Stinging, burning notes
Composing, orchestrating
A song, a chorus
Of a future awakening
To possibilities

Twisted, gnarled branches
Torrential rains
Dayspring, summer flowers
Hot bright scalding light
Tireless efforts revealing
Childhood's dream now in sight

Jackie Davis Allen

with eyes wide open

do you really see the blades of grass, the trees
the leaves beneath the feet of insects, dancing
feasting on the innocence of pollinated flowers
whose scent, the colorful, sings songs of beauty
and you, are you waiting, waiting for Nature's decree
of death of life, are you hoping for a season, or a reason

have you perused the library of the world
traveled near or far beyond the site of your birth
either by land, by sea or by air, or perchance
through the polished lens of the printed word
reflective images spanning the breadth of screens
in living color, or do you live only inside the privacy
of your cocoon, insulated by intimacy's fear

have you tasted the sweetest love, given abundantly
of your treasured time's affection and attention
listened intently, without distraction; been touched and felt
and heard or healed by the sensitive lens of compassion
which sees imperfections, as a mark of all mankind
and, is there any empathy in the world of your making

do you comprehend the importance of being, of seeing
of hearing, of tasting, of feeling, of loving, of caring
and, are there not among us, those, whose days soon
will be reaching the final gasping breath, their final days
stamped with closed eyes; their fists clinched tight
with self-imposed judgment; and I ask, have you
ever lived your life, with eyes wide open?

Life's Breath

As a writer, I wonder
If ever I am to be quoted
As having written anything memorable

Famous quotations are just words

Withstanding the test of time
So, maybe I'll never know
But I'll just keep on writing

As a writer, I dream
Of days gone by, and wonder
Whatever happened to my dreams

Did any of them materialize?

Or did they disappear into the night?
Maybe, I'll never know
Even still, I'll just keep on writing

This one thing, I do know
I must write, it is as important
To me as breath is to life

It is my motivation to continue on

For me, to live is to write
And to write is to live
So, I'll just keep on writing

The Weather's Eye

Against a perilously pink-painted-sky
Seven salty sailors waved their goodbyes
Despite persistent pleading, pathetic sentiments
Onward they sailed, despite the weather's eye

Sailed they the schooner, weathered and worn
Disregarding the past, those left behind
So too their dismay; and like joy, closing its eyes
Mourning is a dark omen had it come to stay

Who is it that painted the sorrowful sky
Why did the sailors wave a final goodbye
Grief, like a thunderstorm, wailed against the night
Wives, lovers, children shrieked, wept and cried

Seasoned, warned, the sailors sailed away
They who were never to return. Like caution
Like winds sweeping over the sea, left behind
Are those who must continue to weather the storm

What He Said

The weekend had arrived, peace
And calm coming like sunshine
Following a week filled with storms

We sat, enjoying brunch, a time
Of refreshment, when to my surprise
He looked at me and said

"To finish my sentence of yesterday . . ."
That is exactly what he said
It is a direct quote

In the shock and surprise of that
Momentous occasion, I forget how
He completed yesterday's comment

Yet, of the time his cranial nerve endings
Took to reconnect, is it not something
To be praised, to be commended?

Alas! The rest of what he said
Has mysteriously found a place to hide
It is buried deep inside of my head

Jackie Davis Allen

A Reminder

Drip, drop. Drip, drop
Steady and sure
Slowly; now, it comes
To a stop
And I fear
I am getting caught up
In the vortex
With nothing left
But swirling accusations
That I am not enough
I have not enough
Of what it takes
To make of my craft
Life's work
But, this one thing
I do know
What I have got
Is the passion
That lights the path
Of my days and nights

Someone Is at the Door

It was late in the bitter, blustery afternoon
The supper table cleared, dishes done
When John Thomas, a kindly old widower
Of some age, heard a knocking at the door

Followed by the sound of shuffling feet
A raspy voice, an animal-like moan, unlike any
John Thomas had ever heard before. It was
Insisting, persisting, demanding entry

Despite the hour, despite an eerie
Whistling of the wind, snow and ice
Greeted John Thomas, when opened
He the door. So surprised was he

Who was it standing there? Cast in snow
And ice, faintly familiar, thought less
Belligerent than ever before, John Thomas
Thought he recognized who it was

His heart was strangely warmed
Thinking the stranger standing there
Might be, in fact, his only son. With a kiss
John Thomas invited him to come inside

The coldness of their relationship melted
Dripping wet with tears of remorse; and
In the knocking and the opening of heart's door
They started out on the path of love once more

Jackie Davis Allen

Time Has Lost All Meaning

Rising in the east is the sun,
A glorious, brilliant presence,
Greeted and welcomed by all.
Yet, waiting for evening time is one
Who would attempt to claim the lovely one.

Shielded by a canopy of anticipation,
The perfume of incense awakens expectation.
It wafts through the air,
Ascends as a young maid's hesitant gift;
Sweet, the scent of euphoria.

For the taste of her lips, the curve of her hips,
He murmurs his sweetest invitation.
And, longing for a taste, breathlessly,
He climbs the evening summit
Then sinks down into the valley.

The night descends into the dawn,
Intoxicated by nature's yearning.
And summoned by her delight,
He claims her ecstasy as his own.
A treasure long-awaited.

Silenced by her receptiveness,
And awarded the bliss of her lips,
She showers on him, her virtuous favor.
Night and day converge; and for them,
Time has lost all meaning.

Not Yet Spring

Bitter cold the day, intensely
The face of the sun spreads its smile
Against a fresh blanket of snow
Fierce winds blowing, swirling

In truth, the chattering wind
Mimics a wild animal's howl
With winter's consent, its bite
Inflicts considerable pain

A bird seen flying high
Up in the unsettled sky
Makes me wonder how it is
That he should suddenly dive

Swiftly down, choosing to rest
On a wire attached
To the decades-old stockade-fence
That has become a good neighbor

What might he be contemplating
Now, as he zooms over and into
The thicket that is the red cedar grove
Might he be considering

That down below, where the snow
Has melted, where earthworms live
An early one might appear
And offer up himself as a sacrifice

Jackie Davis Allen

Buried Treasure

Some days he cannot seem to see
The days pass before him all too quickly
Enshrouded as he is by fog
And, yet he sits before the silence
Where, within, an insistent whisper
Finds him in a meditative trance
His thoughts gathering
And, as through a sifter, now
The minutes, turning into hours

Hours fade into misery's intent
As he ponders his situation
Possibilities, probabilities, neither
Dissipate, nor do they transform
Into reflection but rather
Into a form of contemplation
Spirit lifted, refreshed, inspired
From his inner eye, he clearly sees
Lines lying on the page nearby

Pen and pad, at the ready
Humble instruments, these, his tools
He complies with eager boldness
And, as rescuer, he releases the gifts
Withheld too long from view
Mind-fog, passing, he sees now
How the light of intent emerges
When focused on his gift. Encouraged
And with thanksgiving, he begins anew

Trajectory

Let not the overwhelming profusion
Of dark shadows or the vociferous voices
Presiding over the present day's headlines
Befuddle the calm of your mental faculties.

Abandon not your heart's passionate command!

Remain steadfast as you make your way
Around and over tribulations! For even
Without your consent, the darkness
Will attempt to appropriate its control.

Blink not for a millisecond nor lend attention
To detractors' clamor and rhetoric!
Lest their buffoonery infiltrate your thoughts
And poison your well-thought-out plans.

A laudable soldier continues and marches on.

Arm yourself with truth, cling to your intentions!
Stay alert and heed the warnings!
Yield not to skeptics' gloom and doom!
Too often they are scented with perfume.

Hesitate not, my dear! Make of your heart's path
The personal resolution that burns brightest!
Be on guard! The journey may be fraught
With danger, with obstacles.

Take time to reflect over your declarations!

Jackie Davis Allen

A Vision Beyond the Mountains

I am standing on the front porch, watching the mimosa blossoms wing their way on the backs of the wind, landing here and there. They are painting both, the patches of grass and dirt, a pink and sickly sticky mess. The buzzing of the yellow jackets continues. Undeterred by my annoyance, it is as if the cadence of their insistence silhouettes and shadows the essence of who I am becoming.

I am not quite sure how I know this, but somewhere out there, out in the world beyond these hills, these mountains, there is something more waiting for me. That something, yet to be discovered, will, by necessity, design and become the compass that hopefully guides me on my path to finding out what's in store for me.

The blue of the bead board-ceiling looks down upon the porch swing rocking gently in the wind. Over in the corner, near the banister, above the railing, a starling is busy making a nest. And making a mess on the floor-boards below. And, Poppa, he does not like it if they do that. If he were here, he would take the broom from its corner in the kitchen and let the bird know who is the boss. I cannot remember how many times he has knocked the nest down and how many days the battle waged on until Poppa eventually won. And, the starling, she had to take her home-building skills to a different location.

So, now, I am wearing my Poppa's namesake, and a pair of my cousin's cast-off blue jeans, the ones that make me feel even closer to my father. Whose first name I share. I decide that I best take care of it myself. A few moments later, and the nest will be gone. The interloper, too.

Out on the back porch, I hoist the water bucket down into the well, the rough rope in my hands, listening until I hear it splash, and eventually fills with water. Pulling the rope up is a difficult job and one that I am not supposed to even attempt. But Momma is out at Grandma's and there is no one here to stop me. Momma is always looking at things one way and that way is, someone is going to get hurt.

Of course, it is true that when I lifted the bucket of water out and over the well-box, I could have found myself falling back into the well. Along with the bucket of water.
I guess you could say I never thought that such a thing would happen to me. I carried the water out to the front porch knowing too well, that after I scrubbed up the bird mess, I would have to get the dry mop and take care of the drips I had made carrying the bucket through the kitchen and the living room.

Due to the distance of time, perhaps, I now find myself in moments of solitude glimpsing back into the hollows where I grew up. "Hollers, if you will to those who still carry the dialect." Momma, who has since passed on, once told me something. I hope it is not true, because I do not want to think it is. Anyway, here is what she said. "These are the best days of your life."

Like I implied a minute ago, I did not believe her then and still do not. No disrespect intended. Things happen. To my way of thinking, between Momma and me, it always depended upon who it was that was doing the thinking.

Memory images pass by, though faded a bit. Tattered and torn. And yet, some are in living color. When I used to sit back there in the darkened theater, I felt as if I was watching black and white newsreels depicting a strange and foreign reality. Later, I came to understand that those black and white films of "the olden days", were less than a decade older than I. Searching the faces of the soldiers, looking for my father, always, during the theater's newsreels was difficult. I never found him. It would be decades later, after he had passed on that I discovered he had served under General Patton in North Africa. Later, too, was when I learned that much of my childhood had been colored by the anxieties of my parents.

As a daughter of a coal-miner and a stay at home-mother, life would find me with nine siblings and the sureness that life is not forever. Death hovered over life and what a cruel discovery that has been when I first tasted it within my own family. Three infant siblings. So sad, dying so young. As a child, sleep eluded me. I counted sheep. They jumped over the promises, whose numbers should have rescued me. Like my "Our Father's" and "Now I Lay Me Down's", they fused into the whole of darkness that sank down around the foothills where I lived. Eventually, I would fall asleep. Though I thought I never would.

Despite, or perhaps because of the wailing of the steam-powered locomotive that ran along the railroad tracks across the way, the night fueled my imagination. Held hostage by the closeness of those same mountains, my imagination joined a host of counting sheep and the many prayers uttered, until finally, exhausted, I would fall into a fitful sleep. Beseeching God became a nightly ritual as was being abruptly awakened most mornings by a scruffy scratching on my cheek.

Grandpa shaved only on Friday evenings. He, believing in the Scriptures, held with not working on the Sabbath. That meant he best get out the straight edge and give himself a clean shave so as to be ready to head on down the road to the Baptist church in time for services, come Saturday morning. And, so, kissing me, he would wake me up. "Wake up, sleepy head! You're missing the best part of the day. Come on, I need your help."

I did not think so. But I was awake. And, Grandpa needed me to help him. Long retired from coal-mining, he and Grandma had both a kitchen-garden as well as their fields up in the mountains. There, where they grew a large assortment of vegetables, sharing with my family the apples, pears and black walnuts that grew in abundance.

The strawberry-patch was situated up in the fields, down by the mountain-stream. As you might have guessed, it was a favorite spot of mine. Much to the consternation of my grandmother who reminded me, "I'm saving the strawberries" . . . to make jam, or a pie, or some such excuse, she, always warning me not to be over-zealous in my sampling. But, oh, were those strawberries sweet!

With stains of the night riding on my shoulders, and infantile sleep bugs still nestling in my eyes, I greeted Grandpa, though not with a welcome. "It is too early . . ." Not to be denied, my protestations ignored, Grandpa continued, "As soon as you eat your breakfast, I need you to come on up to the fields and help me hoe the corn."

Grandpa always walked into our house, never knocking. The front door was always unlocked as were all the doors to the houses in our neighborhood. In response to my mother's comment about the skeleton-key, I rolled my eyes. "Everyone's door opens with the same-skeleton key. So, there is no need for us to lock our door." So, we did not. And, no one else did either.

After delivering a brief message, my grandfather always, yes, always, walked out the back door. I thought that mighty strange then and still do. Yet, that was his routine. Always in the front door. And out the back door. Try as I may, contrary to Grandma's routine, I can never ever remember Grandpa taking the time to sit down when he came out to our house. He just came in and went back out, taking only the amount of time to deliver his message.

Neither did Grandpa ever sit down on the front porch-swing, or in one of the gliders. Or, for that matter, even on the couch in our living room. I was, perhaps, ten years old when the couch and chair in our living room were new, relatives of the ones in his living room. Only the colors were different. His were maroon and ours blue. I thought they were velvet. Maybe they were mohair? Anyway, they had wide upholstered arms with wide wooden carved and varnished shiny fingers. Sort of strange . . . fingers on the arms of furniture.

That Grandpa never ate a meal that was not at his own kitchen table, one prepared by Grandma on the wood-fired cookstove, regardless of the weather, goes without saying. Why that was so, I do not know. If ever I asked him, I do not remember now. Out of respect, the way I was brought up, I probably never thought to ask him. Grandpa just had a way of doing things. Doing them his way.

Building Up, Tearing Down

Pride hath ways, mostly overbearing
Loves whom he has become
Rejoices when others fall flat on their face

Finds self difficult to see as others do
The butt of jokes, laughed at behind the back
He, a sad clown fools no one but self

Perchance, he comes to worry about the cost
Of self-worth, falling off pages of a fairy tale
Constructed from fancy, counting cards

Caring not the cost, the price
Neither yields old fallacies
That once propped him up

Why he knows not to lock doors to charade
To seal all cracks in that pathetic facade
Why he buries not his shameful face in disgrace

And why he has no eyes to see a high place
Of illusion where a circus of fools
Walk fine lines just like he, himself

Like nightfall, and sure as certain
He relinquishes neither pride nor ego
Still walks on the high wire of deception

In tenuous moments, appeased
Indulgently pleased with hot air
Of self-importance

Yet would not be a greater act
To wipe off inferiority's old mask
Remove the complex of superiority

Jackie Davis Allen

And step down a greater man
To begin rejuvenation's work
Of building up self and others

In need of constant attention
Will he yet remain a sad clown, puffed up
With pride, destined to fall on his disgraced face

Prideful excess weighs down shades
Of still greater a loss, so blinded is he to truth
He keeps playing the same old maiming games

Sweet Molly

Molly was, at the age of precociousness
Sitting in the swing, on the front-porch
Of her rural mountain-home

She was dreaming of possibilities
Fantasizing about opportunities

And, Molly, bored beyond tears
Looked deep into the eye
Of her imagination, and saw golden fields

The wheat fields introduced themselves
As children, desirous of her company

Sweet Molly. She listened intently
As the restless wind issued an invitation
It was waving a welcome, encouraging her

It was as if her dream had come true
On the truest-blue of crystal-clear days

Curious, expectant, our dearest Molly
Lunging eagerly, excitedly latched onto
The beribboned kite-tail of a rainbow

Jackie Davis Allen

Waiting for Winter

It is cool and bright in the blue mountains.
The deep chill of night has moved, settled
Down into the valley.

The morning sun spreads
Her arms over and around, painting
In autumn's colors. It is a gift.

Still, quiet, peaceful-like, I walk
Around leaves. Yellow, red, rust, and brown.
Many have fallen to the welcoming ground,

Protection's blanket for nature's seedlings.
It is season's own version of a healthy need
To relax, contemplate and to hibernate.

My heart skips to the tune of Earth's blessings.
I am singing a song. The stanzas, not formed.
Neither a note, upon a page.

Or played by musicians, nor ever sung
By any, except by those who dare
To leave behind the world's loud clamors.

I welcome you, o, peaceful morning!
Your gift of joy is mine. Rest, relief you bring
To my soul. You remind me to shine,

To shine on one and all. You, I embrace
And, unlike the sun who asks for nothing
I ask, I pray God, may the world be at peace.

No Illusions . . . through the looking glass

More than Meets the Eye

Ah, it's no fun to wash the dishes!
Can't sister do them, just this one time?
I've so many books to read, dreams to dream.

I need to travel somewhere in my mind.
A knock at the door. Oh, it's you know who!

He wants to play. Walks in. Assured, confident
Says, let's go to the movies. And I think, no way,
It's my turn to do the dishes.

Shouldn't want to ask sister, wouldn't want
To impose, or neglect my responsibility.

A voice enters the room, so loud it seems
That my excuse is blown out of the way.
Go on ahead! Run along and enjoy the day!

And, resisting to no avail, I'm thinking,
No summer plaything will I be

Nor a flower in anyone's lapel
Nor will I be viewed as summer-stock.
I'll exert myself one of these days.

Now, he's parking the car, checking beneath
The hood. Returns. Attempts to check me out.

Summer's over. He's back at school. So glad.
But, have you heard the news? You Know Who
Has up and got himself married!

Caught Up

Wandering down the aisles
Perusing the offerings
Checking my wish-list
Against my bank account

Waiting for discernment
Waiting, too, for the treasures
Which ones to purchase
Which ones to leave behind

Meandering through the mall
Enticing scents and flavors
Music to soothe the senses
Alas! I have exceeded my limit

Resting now, my weary feet
Taking care of my aching back
Putting off until tomorrow
All the things I must take back

Determined

I will go now, down from the mountains

My freedom before me, the chains
Of poverty loosened, my thoughts
Soaring over valleys, hills, dales
Into the future, awaiting

I promise, this is my manifesto

Naysayers will choke one day
On their prognostications
They, humbled; they, cowering
Leveled beneath shock and awe

When the day has come, drawn near

Return with me to the place
Where inspiration breathed hope
Where will, effort and perseverance
Lifted me up, over and beyond

Novel

Mysterious
Strange
Clashing
Personalities
Secrets
Revealed
Consequences
Paid
Creating
Unfolding
Revealed now
The novel

In Step with Fashion

Beneath the light of the photographer's flash

She is a fashion maven, a facade of her youth
She focuses her newly-arranged eyes
On the curious strut of the avant-garde
Anorexic and abnormally thin
Perched on antique chairs with fragile legs

Sitting demurely, glaring at the others

As brilliantly adorned as she, she sighs
In heightened exaggeration, faun of excitement
Hiding behind a signature of self-absorption
Behind scenes of stress and anxiety, she reigns
As frantic designers, frenetically, scurry around

Aspiring assistants primp and prep

Her paper doll-image, a magazine cut-out
This marvelous maven, heavily-perfumed
Seeks something to transform her
That, unlike the blue jay's cry, will deceive
The irrationality of her grandiose imagination

With wrinkles tucked behind ears, she wears

The colors of her years, along with hair
Camouflaged to match the haute couture
Of famous names. She stands out
From the crowd. She conceals a frown
Seems that all her peers have been similarly
Commercially altered, transformed

Jackie Davis Allen

Patience

Past trepidation, she searched
The recesses of her heart
And there, waiting, tucked back

Behind the black and blue stains

Of sorrow and sadness
She discovered gifts hiding
Gifts, pregnant with promise

They, yearning to be given birth

She was like a neglected bud
That failed to live up to its promise
Yet, with acceptance

She began to spend time and effort

Loving and forgiving herself, others
Though some weed-like stains remain
She scents her days with patience

So Many Questions

There are so many questions when
A pontificator spouts with illusion, flowing
From the fount of her mouth.

Oh, yes! There are so many questions
As to what happened.

Attired in buffoonery's prideful perception,
Claiming she bears no blame, no shame,
With delusion, she fashions a piece of fiction.

She exploits the failure of her game,
Presumes we do not know what happened.

She denies fabrication of partisan events,
Excoriates adversaries, and rising to the top
Of persona non grata's incompetence,

She extracts a price to kiss her hand.
So, do you want to know what happened?

Is not the answer as plain
As the nose on Pinocchio's face?
Or, perhaps, that does not fit the narrative . . .

There are so many other questions.
Like, how does she reconcile the night?

Jackie Davis Allen

Battle-Weary

With spring, comes the rain, torrents
Pouring down all around, and despite
All my efforts, I am being attacked
By an enemy, a swarm of many

They fly, intent upon destination
Seeking to refuel at any cost
Wings widespread, they come with stealth
Necessity, providing a landing pad

Unconcerned, for the damage they cause
The dreaded females circle day and night
They seek blood, persistent in desire
To attack, despite the risk of their own demise

First-aid rendered, returned to attack mode.
Determined to win, I am crouching low, seizing
The moment, chasing the vicious mosquito
The one that led the blood-letting attack

Contagious

The waiting room is filled. Funeral parlor, quiet
And the single practitioner is already late
By over half an hour; so, what is new? I try not
To look at the clock. So, I pick up a magazine

We, the others, they, like I, are waiting, each one of us
Harboring individual, personal, private health-issues
Across the room, there is another perusing a magazine
He looks up. Well, hey! How's everyone today?

From my magazine, I look up. Surprised, startled
To hear anyone other than the medical staff speaking
A young man, to my right, laughs self-consciously
I'm sick. How about you?

I guess I am doing o.k., that is, for an old man
This coming from one less than half my age
I guess none of us is feeling all that well
Or else, we would not be sitting where we are

Seeing an opening, I cannot resist
Age has nothing to do with it. I am a writer
Getting ready to publish my third book
I pass around my business cards. Poetry

The room grows quiet. Like an empty funeral parlor
Except one who says he will check me out on the web
Anyway, I am hoping the news of my authorship
Will spread like a contagious cold

Jackie Davis Allen

a million stars in the sky

the salty breeze kisses the night with the gentle art of
passion's melody and with heart's rising and sighing
it is as if I am looking at love's reflective shore
the dawn, hiding her face from the sandy beach

the saltwater-tides rise and fall
the crashing waves, too, in syncopation
with the lovers; their songs, familiar

they mimic the wind's wild cry
they caress the sea-foam's froth-kissed mist
in passion's blissful estate; they bathe,
thinking of nothing other than intimacy's gift
love guides their innocent, wistful wishes

they thought then, they think now,
they were witnessing a million stars
waking up the sky

This Side of Heaven

He is inside his condo, on the fifteenth floor
The chairs on the balcony, empty, waiting
He is toying with words, fidgeting with keys
The means to exercise his frenetic energy

The air-conditioning unit pauses, yawns

Be it high-tide, wide or low, it matters not
To the cruise ships maneuvering beyond
Tiny lights flickering, how they diminish now
The ocean, waving wild, white foam, frothing

It is one way to pass the time

In the distance, brushing up against the sky
A cargo ship appears as if a young child
Has cut and pasted its image in miniature
On a piece of paper, construction-gray

A yellow ball sinks down into the blue-green

He is reconciling more than this, as he arranges
The navy's training jets and seagulls against
The empty seats on the balcony, the table, life
Missing the love of his life, he rises from bed

And considers how the story should end

Jackie Davis Allen

Incomprehensible

The day gasped, damp moss, dank, dark
And sweet; the earth, opening six feet below
Waiting with the face of conceit

Mourning clothes, silk and satin
A black veil I had bought, death and loss
Colored uneasy my woebegone thoughts

Carved out of love, by his father
From ancient mountain's boulders, the coffin
Borne above, on grieving, heaving shoulders

Grief rained, streaked, salting down
My tormented face against the eulogy
Of my beloved who had lost the race

He lies there alone, cold, unable
To acknowledge me, family, and yes, friends
All those paying homage

Weeping now, they for the one who has passed
His grave lies so silently
The dark clouds increase, unsurpassed

Obscure they, the star of the Sun
A day punctuated like an accent mark
Yet, he left his endearing mark

Like flowers wilting in place, brief in scent
His life met not its intent, three decades in span
His was an abbreviated existence

No Illusions . . . through the looking glass

Between Darkness and Dawn

The deep eye of the wind-swept-sky watched
While the silent stars lent their countenance
Communicating their light on the silhouettes

Bare-branched trees randomly thrashed
Against the angst of his turmoil

Sleep found him not. Weary, concerned
Troubled, disquieted, he, on his knees
Praying, seeking pardon, and waiting

He groaned, pleaded for courage
For the fortitude of compassion, for its leniency

And lifting himself up, he climbed into bed
And began to navigate the waters
In the darkness of his soul, a developing mystery

As in a dream, he sees someone
Familiar, someone older, someone desperate

Someone at loose ends, prepared to relinquish
Ready to turn away from his errant ways
Dawn finds him with a smile on his face

Jackie Davis Allen

Say, It Isn't So!

She announced that she was ready
Openly lying in wait, awake
Face and name, widely disseminating blame
She, caring less than what she said frightened
What few friends she had remaining

Posters in black-and-white and in color
Emblazoned with deceptive face
Presented her character as pristine, spotless
Her fame as stellar as was the platform
On which she spouted her leanings

A physician said that she was drowning
The stagnant waters were deep and putrid
Where she swam, and like a flailing fish
Flipping and flopping, she was unable
To sleep, afraid she might not awaken

Her head ached, the truth was the only prescription
Yet, she chose to let her mind bleed out. Too late
To seek help. It is said she alienated all
Even as she, to no avail, begged, pleaded
For anyone, for someone to prop her up

As from the vitriol she spawned, she lay
In its bile, staining the once-pristine sheets
Foul were the quotations, memory's sad mimicry
Despite lamentations, she attempted to smile
Yet, found it impossible to look into the mirror

Alas! I Am the Mother

She was not on the bus. Where is my daughter?
What has happened to her? I am beside myself
She is missing. I am crying, wringing my hands
Trying to remember what she was wearing
When she left for school this morning.

Someone is at the door, someone I do not recognize.
She appears considerable older than my daughter
Though she looks faintly familiar. I cannot
Place her amongst my daughter's friends.
She rushes past me; runs up the stairs.

I am stunned, shocked, my mouth hangs open.
Who is this brash teenager, the one acting
Strangely familiar? She, the one wearing
Pants so tight they seem like a second skin, a fishnet
Blouse, a leather vest. I cannot catch my breath.

The fringe above, below her eyes is black, it flutters
Beneath green eyes. Her glasses are a garish blue.
Her ivory skin sports two red splotches, her hair
Bleached blond with extensions. She is an intruder.
Like her ruby stained lips, I am aghast.

I am following her upstairs. But what am I to do?
I hear the phone ring, pick it up, say hello.
Her father is on the other end. What I am about
To tell him will send his voice up several octaves.
He is apoplectic, his voice strained.

Jackie Davis Allen

In My Dreams

Waves ripple the lily pond, lemon-lime
Vines caress, carelessly, a nearby fence.
The Sun, soothingly, strokes the landscape
Plays host to shadow's dark dance.
I feel like an intruder.

Unexpectedly, cool is summer's breeze.
Silhouetted against the searing Sun's heat,
A dog anxiously barks in the background,
Disrupting my desired sense of calm.
Out of necessity, I readjust my priorities.

Quiet returns, invites courage to participate,
To join in meditation, to hear the bird's song,
To commune with one's self, to forgive
The inventory received, its perceived wrongs.
I drink in the glory that is the morning.

Lacy patterns paint the grove of trees.
Their leaves snuggle against the sky's blue hues,
Like a stalwart sentry, serendipity
Spreads a canopy of peace, just for me.
The thread-leaf maple smiles, encouragingly.

Climbing white roses mingle with pink and red.
St. John's Wort's stoically ponders the scene.
Pregnant, the butterfly-bush awaits the day
Of the butterflies, bees and hummingbirds.
In my garden of dreams, I am never alone.

No Illusions ... *through the looking glass*

Something

Something there is
That is not, something that was
Not quite as I had expected.

I heard a knock, or what I thought, something
Or someone was banging on my door.
Yet, nothing to my eyes did appear.

Slamming tight the door,
I shut it against, along with my fear.
With a key, I double-locked it.

And still, I heard something.
Something terrible at my door.
Something like I had never heard before.

Then, surprised was I to see
When morning awakened me, clock-springs
Scattered across the hardwood floor.

Unraveled, unnerved, I further saw
My bedroom door flung open against
The wall. I was trembling inside.

Sometimes, there happens to happen
A mystery, and though we try as try we may
It to decipher, the mystery remains unsolved.

Jackie Davis Allen

What to Do?

Declutter, but how am I
To choose what to let go?
Go to the closet, take a look
Close the door, change my mind.

I think I will leave it for a later time.
Renovate, but first, what to do?

How to accomplish the goal?
Check out a fishing site, buy
Some worms, spend the day
Contemplating what next to do.

Tomorrow's on my calendar, a note
So too, a things to-do-list.

But decluttering
Is so hard to do. Perhaps, I will choose
To sit down, or take a nap and forget
About what I need to do.

A Song of Lamentation and Hope

O sad heart
Be still thy instrument
Of dark mystery
Like stealth of night
Like wolf on prowl
In the dark of the night
Misery finds no relief
In restless sleep
Whether it be a bright day
Or the darkest of nights
Like lost stars, moon
Like lost desire
My life requires
Your touch, your love
Desolation to repeal
O console my memory
Come now with haste
Fill my heart's hunger
Quench my thirst
Come now with harp and song
Bring your sweetest wine
Dearest one
Wherever you are
Whatever the weather
Be thou mindful
I adore you, I miss you
My love, I implore you
Find your way home

They Begged for More

Old Natas smiles, bestows upon those in need
Gifts, grants them a full measure of greed
Awash in propaganda's ink, the sheep fall
Beneath illusion's spell and guile's wink

Old Natas, admired by sheep as a god
Cares neither for respect or truth's regard
He goes forth, reviling, demeaning
Effort's hard work, responsibility

Claims he, as his own, a rogue's role
One with the mind of complete control
The sheep, encouraged by manipulation
Parrot the flames of his heretical ire

Devoid of heart's consciousness
With attitude of malfeasance
Old Natas rules with disingenuous intent
Disburses evil by way of his sheep

His brand of deception comes with demands
Think not, just bury your head in the sand
He pontificates to subservient throngs
Applaud, they, the one to whom they belong

fissures of futility

the fuse
of functional fictionality
framed the form
of the book he was writing
for the cover, the book jacket
on which was featured a torch

the agitated author
certainly, was no match
for the dire
and distressing disturbances
created by a detractor
to whom a debt was owed

determined to deny
for the other any compensation
they destroyed each other's reputation
insuring one's literary demise
thus, preventing either one
from receiving a single, solitary cent

Jackie Davis Allen

An Appalachian Saga

It did not begin in 1915, but that's where we will start the saga of a young couple, both born in 1897. On the threshold of awakening desire, their love ignited the flame of their lives, they residing in the mountains of Appalachia. Marching to the drumbeat of their hearts, weathering together days of raging storms, sunny days, and burning nights of shared passion, love fueled their existence. Their first years were filled with exploring one another, merging love and life until the evil, the unbelievable, the Great War of 1917 raised its ugly head.

The horrors, the fears were so great that the unnamed soldier, so battle-worn, later denied he had ever served in the Great War. The means to his survival. Night visions, the only proof. Grim determination became the sad portrait of the two, when the Grim Reaper claimed precious infant ones and dear relatives. Death marched darkly into their world with the evil of the 1918 Influenza Pandemic-war. More than fifty million met their fate that way, carried off before their time to the great beyond. The world knelt down in grief. Such were the circumstances of that time.

Aged beyond their physical years, scarred by labor, uncertainty, the grief-stricken couple rose at four to toil in the morning. Sustaining life as farmers, the couple resolutely arched their backs, determined. Up and back down the mountain-trail, they walked to their gardens, calling them "fields". Accompanied by mule and cart. They soldiered and disciplined themselves while marshaling produce, filling winter's larder with the tools of sharpened hoes, bent back, with necessity. With purpose. Chopping wood, hauling coal, carting water from the cold water-stream, heated in tin tubs by outdoors fire; clothes scrubbed, lye soap awaiting washboard's cleansing efforts.

Knuckles bled and worked themselves to the bone. Such back-breaking work lulled them to bed by six, the soldier-farmers, awakening by dawn's cock-a-doodle-do to start it all over again. Sustenance-living was the General who urged them ever onward. Battles fought with dangerous snares and toil, the enemies, snaking and stalking. Still, they labored, daily, eking out a living. Provisions from the soil, planting, tilling, hoeing, harvesting and carting it back down to their family's house. Caring for panting mules and sun scorched-bodies, repeating the life their parents had known. Stoking fires, both with wood and coal, feeding animals, and the children of which now numbered two. Life's journey with the war of existence continued.

Cold treacherous winters, roads narrow and gutted, traversed only in emergency, on horseback or on foot. Necessity stretched the larder until spring returned again. They leaned on one another as the Great Depression claimed its victims. Needs became insurmountable, forcing old and young men alike to search the uniform of coal-miners or the lumbermen, they, enlisting for whatever pittance they might receive. Bills had to be paid. And, all the people of the Cumberland Mountains, ever so resourceful, hunkered down in dress of victorious uniform, triumphing over unknown wants. They were a resilient army of people.

Growing offspring resisted, sometimes militantly. Deciding for themselves to desert their superiors, some marrying young, others joining the service, clinging to hope. All, praying to God that World War II would soon be over. The death tallies and deprivations continued. Daily were the reminders of those missing or captured by the enemy, broadcast by a neighbor, the radio and in the theaters, and by telegram. The news stabbed their hearts and gave rise to the supporting of the effort to stop the insanity. The evil that was led by the madman, Hitler.

The men rallied to support the effort, yet, they longed

for someone to return home to. To give them hope and a reason to live. Still, they assembled and marched off to war, leaving behind parents, siblings, children, mothers, fathers. Some left wives of one day; infants on the way.

The men were brave. Some never would return or be seen again. Treasured letters and photos kept alive the spirit of who they were, lovers of peace called to destroy the threat.

War changed everything. Women left behind picked up the pieces of life once headed by men. Women, now working outside of the hearth grew in confidence as they produced weapons and materials for their countrymen. All prayed for the war's end. Would it ever end? Anxiety rode on worker's backs as they fastened the rivets onto machines that traveled in places women could not go, even in their minds. The church pews overflowed. The sturdy mountaineers prayed for peace.

Once the war was over and things returned to normal, they really did not return to normal. That is, if they did return and had not been killed or wounded in battle. Men found wives and girlfriends different, in ways their own differences did not compute. Some men were missing limbs. Others, their minds. Still, others were missing comrades who died before their eyes. Holding back the flood as best they could, asking God, "Why was I the one to survive?" Questions were asked, and sometimes answered, and not always to satisfaction: "How can I know this baby's mine?"

Challenged wives and girlfriends sometimes abandoned all hope while their men were off fighting for Uncle Sam. Some women turned to left-behind men while soldier lovers, reduced, read "Dear John"-letters.

Heartaches and hurt aches remained for the survivors of war. Often estranged by unspeakable horrors, reunited or rejected as strangers, even still, many clung to one another, so as to carve out a new way of living for themselves. In the aftermath of war's evil, the men tried to find their place.

Women often were put back in their place. The church offered solace to those who came.

The days and years marched on, and work claimed its place in the lives of the changed people of the Cumberland Mountains of Appalachia. Coal was king for a while. Times were sometimes good but mostly hard. Anxiety reigned either from fear of their men, sons or husbands losing their jobs or getting injured, perhaps losing their lives. Women worried and did what they could.

That changed women considered taking on paying jobs unsettled many men's minds. Yet, often it was necessary. Food and shelter, and medical care won out. And life in the mountains marched on. Hunger was the new battle for all of them, men, women, children.

The sharp prices of seeds, the need for organic fertilizer and sawdust to improve the land called forth for renumeration to those who owned the stores. Often, both parents worked for pay if they could. Women of the mountain who once stayed home cooking, sewing, canning, and more were seen out in the world seeing and wanting more. A paycheck made it all worthwhile. The expense of losing a way of life. A new anxiety took up residence in the lives of those living in the mountains and hollers.

All the while, the goal was improvement. Sadly, lagging confidence became the key that locked so many into place. Education and the coming decades were the solutions that would release meaningful opportunities. Fortunate were the children and grandchildren of the different wars, they, who were privileged to attend college on scholarships. They left with grand ideas of returning and teaching and giving back, only to discover instead a life within their reach with less hardship and more adventure. With the coveted diploma in hand, some marched off to the city. A marriage license and a career, leading the way.

Granddaughters of the mountain, now married with

children of their own, faced a juggling act with choices difficult to make. Staying home or going to work. Grandparents could only shake their heads. The cities claimed many a mountain-child because education's ticket offered something more. Still, life's journey continued. Greater expectations took root in coal-mining descendants. Many chose not to return to the mountains.

    Mountain life changed forever as coal and timber were exhausted. And, age, health and loss of hope sometimes followed. Not all the youth chose to leave, or could.

One Man's Story

His heart is etched like a battlefield, damaged by the scarred grave of his lost youth. Long days and nights, thundering with exploitation, he dreams to deny the ravages of war. He struggles. Yet, the movie plays on, in his mind.

Still, beneath the all-knowing skies, nightmares solemnly screech their mournful cries, echoing his daytime soulful, heart rending songs.

Silenced by ominous shadows, the slime serpent imprints a tattooed stain on his mind. Waves of memory, willfully, wash upon the beach of time. He feels so alone.

The sun rises. Rain dutifully falls. A rainbow appears to bestow a promise. But, blinded by the nettles of pain, everything but the roar of the ocean seems to be the same.

Holding hope in his hands, he is praying to be led by God's grace to go beyond the pain into a calm and comfortable place. Exhausted from copious confession and tears for forgiveness received, he bows on bended knee and prays.

Thank you for bringing me home. Though unworthy I be, please help me to find a way to remove the stains of horror, lest I be of no service to you.

Do with me as you please.

Jackie Davis Allen

The Way It Used to Be

When she was a child, a noted author wrote that she had to pull the covers up over her head at night, so as to keep the mice from nibbling on her ears. One night, when I heard what I guessed were the warning, scratching sounds of a mouse, I did just what the writer had done. I pulled the covers up over my head.

 The cool air-return-duct, in the corner of my bedroom, led up from the coal- and wood-fired furnace, recently installed in the basement. That was the source of where the sounds were coming from. Mice performed their acrobatic acts at night, it seemed, when I was the only one still awake. Least wise, no one else professed to know anything about the night performers. That left me feeling all alone.

 The holes in the grate of the cool-air-return were large enough for a mouse to get through. However, I often heard the mouse sliding back down the insides of the air-duct. I just knew, however, and for certain, that one of these days or nights, a mouse would find a way out of that air-duct. Pulling the quilts over my head would be no deterrent to their determined antics. Even so, most nights, I pulled the quilts up over my head, just in case, and tried to drown out the agonizing sounds. I tried saying every prayer that I had ever memorized, and some of my own. I also counted sheep. Come morning, I was always surprised to find myself awakening to Blue Grass Music on the radio. It was not the music that surprised me. It was the fact that I suddenly realized I had actually slept the previous night. And, my ears were intact. But, then, there was always another night and another night. And, another.

 My bedroom was not actually my own. I shared it with my siblings, they, varying in number, sex and size depending upon the year. When we first moved into our newly stick-built house, a couple of years back, it consisted of four rooms. Each room was exactly the same size, twelve feet by twelve feet. Now, we had six rooms, adding two extra bedrooms because our family kept growing. The room I shared with my siblings contained two beds; both were what is called "full size". With metal springs, a lumpy mattress was placed on top. I searched my memory, choked up a couple of times, when I remembered. That same room once held not only those beds but a baby bed. And a dresser. One of the dresser drawers held the twins. The ones that lived only a short while.

    I am not sure the word "insulation" had found its way into the vocabulary of the builders, one of whom was my uncle. He married one of my mother's sisters. The space between the wall and the window-frame was filled with newspapers and rags to keep out the cold. It did not work very well. It is but a faint memory, but one that I definitely remember. Why, I wonder, did they not make windows that were flush with the walls?

    Those same windows had sheer curtain panels hanging over each. My father nailed the panels to the top of the window-frames, using little black tacks with large heads. When Momma saw fit to wash the panels, she had to pull out the tacks with a claw-hammer and place the lacy panels in the washtub to soak. Lye-soap did the job for both clothes and bodies. A bit rough. But that is what we had. When idle, the washtub and the wash-board hung on nails driven into the wall of the back-porch. The back-porch was just steps away from the kitchen. A portion of which later became a place to store salt-pork when my grandfather slaughtered a hog.

    Sleep came fitfully. Sometimes, when my father came home from work, I would still be awake. Through the thin walls, I could hear my parents in the kitchen. From past experiences, I knew they would be emptying the pots of hot water simmering on top of the cookstove into the tin tub so my father could try to wash away all the coal-dust. The coal-dust that was inside of him, stayed inside of him. That was what caused him to have trouble breathing. The doctors called it "Black Lung." No way to wash it out.

It was with him to the very end.

No Illusions . . . through the looking glass

A Party to Attend

Sifting down, thick fog, snowy-white
A damsel in distress
Awaits a long-awaited scene
She is dreaming of dancing
At the Gala, at the Ball

Hazardous, treacherous
Black ice, the villain

The roads, too difficult for the car
To navigate. Glass slippers, unfit to traverse
The path to where she would dance
With her handsome escort

Outside her window
Snow thickens like cream

What to do? No fairy godmothers
To summon to her rescue
To transport her safely
To where the holiday-lights gleam

Wearing a brocaded gown
And a bejeweled tiara

But wait. The fog lifts
The landscape is a dream
The man in the moon smiles
His approval. So, let the party begin

Jackie Davis Allen

Grace, Sweet Grace

Two childhood friends
Each choosing a different path
Converged upon a stage
By means of serendipity
And, one, as a stranger meeting
A long-lost friend, coveted
The other's place in the spotlight

When the other, I suppose
As well as he may, embraced not
This stranger-friend's fame
He wondered, little comprehending
How the other's kindness
His generosity was so easily
Forthcoming, overflowing

And humbled, one
By the meeting with the other
One chose to shake the other's hand
And in utmost sincerity
Offered up his congratulations
Commending him to others
As his newest old friend

It would be a mistake
If you were not informed
Of the greater significance
Of this mysterious incident
For it was Grace who nudged the one
To step aside. It was then that each could
Revel in the other's limelight

Innocence Lost

While traveling on life's highway
The windows of her eyes
Revealed such amazing sights
Ones she had never seen before
Of so many different peoples, here and there
Diverse as the colors of the rainbow
People and scenes passing by,
Like none of the others
She had ever seen before

She wore a mask
Which concealed her trepidation
The others wore theirs as well
For whatever was their reason
All appeared as props, yet, strange
Were the characters in living color
Who moved as if in a silent movie
Each intent upon their own thoughts

Still, a pleasant scene, expected, unlike
Down the road, the tires rolled noisily
As she took notes, quietly playing her part

She arrived on time
The stage was as described
Bustling with scrambling activity
Then, smelling the scent of danger
Her mask slipped, and her purse
She tucked tightly beneath her arm
Dragging her overnight-bag behind her

Terrified, she withdrew
And, backed up against the wall
Against the door, she pressed her foot forward

Jackie Davis Allen

As hands, forbidden hands, reached in
Found her and began invading
Touching, taking, laughing

She fought, cried, prayed and waited
Hoping he would answer the phone
She was aghast, frightened even
After the thugs had fled
Wondering why it was that she
Was the one that had been accosted

Now, hysteria replaced her puzzlement
Over the changes in the script
As she mourned the loss of her possessions
Her dignity, and so much more

It seemed the ringing went on for hours
And hours, an impotent siren with flashing lights
Whirling, wailing, in her mind
But to no succoring avail, until her lover
Awakened by the call, finally
Picked up the crying, pleading instrument

Only then was it that the invisible distant
Line connected them and clearly
Communicated the late-hour horror
That she, inside a telephone booth
Painted with loud and colorful graffiti
Was waiting, trapped, and still ever so afraid
For the scent of the evil ones
Had not yet dissipated

A Moving Exposition

Beneath, where man cannot see
The ocean-deep is alive
It is an artist's palate, filled
With nature's creation

It is a moving exposition
That few are able to experience
Unless, and if only
They adorn a submersible gear

More than the mind can conceive
The ocean presents
Images, colors that rival those
Of the most-gifted artists

Vibrantly alive, its waters hold
A smorgasbord of delight
A mystery that only God
The master architect, could design

Jackie Davis Allen

It Happened that . . .

A coin fell between the cracks
Beneath the porch, where in its silence
It offered up not a single sound

Neither, when a little child
Seen picking up the treasure, found
The courage to save it, to pocket it
Against a foreboding day of tears

Against a cloud of unforgiving fears
A lone mocking bird fell off the track
The creature losing its former balance

Mocked he, with persistence, the other birds
Always, as always was his style
Believing he was forever bound
To attack. He attacked, and committed

All the rest of his remaining years
To the challenging of all of his peers,
So too a monarch who caught a lot of flack

His Louis Vuitton, he filled with malice
And later, wondering why he had incurred
Derision, discovered he was greatly reviled
For decades no one had ever found a way

Nor the courage to make him lose it
And now that he was old and scared
He questioned why he was so unprepared

A To-Do-List

Be inclusive
Sing, dance
Laugh uproariously
Make time for friends
For self
Be a friend
Forsake the pursuit
Of material things
The unnecessary

Take time to live
To fully enjoy
Love one another
Share generously
Do what is right
Love, both in word
And in deed
A tender heart dances
So, dance

Have mercy, sow seeds
Follow the kindness-path
Forgive others
Self, too, and often
Remember to affirm
The best of yourself
Claim as your mantra
With God's help, I will
Do the best that I can

Jackie Davis Allen

Mirror of Reflection

From the harsh bed of discontent, I rose up
And, with purpose, took down
From time's creative shelf
The dusty tools, thirsting to be spent
As I began to sketch a likeness, a portrait
Of myself, I looked deep into the well

I saw a shadowy reflection staring
Back at me. It was dark with excuses
With features not unlike those of my own
Motivated by fear, desire washed my face
Clean of any past
Then to God, I gave thanks

I made note of some plans to better myself
To improve my lot. Endowed with pockets
Generously filled with promise
I invested lavishly, determining
Never again shall I pretend
That I am what I am not

With help in self-improvement
I became a work in progress
I ignored all the what if's
And with relief, I buried them in the sand
Now, the value of my days is measured
By how poetry guides my willing pen

A Literary Encounter

After a time of refreshment
Three good friends sat, intimately sharing
Enjoying poetry, listening to one
Whose expressive eloquence
Mirrored that of the poet

Beneath the impressionistic pages
Metaphors, similes yielded views, picturesque
Revealed, too, were truths broader
Than those placed in the original's
Black-and-white-script

Eloquence's rosy face emerged
From lines, verses articulated with passion
Each reliving, echoing something
From the past, the present; the future
On the verge of an awe-struck revelation

With hearts, minds undivided
Unencumbered, we shared ourselves
And embracing the moment, reluctant
To return back to Earth
We grew transparent wings

With passionate fervor
We flew higher than ever before
Know this: It was no ordinary encounter
Rather, it was like night, transformed unto day
Believe me, it was a life-empowering experience

soberly, seriously

like the winter-season
where trees with bare branches stand
like the revelers
who celebrate the warmth of the bottle
inebriated, they stagger throughout the land
everyone, struggling under the influence
the acrid scent of the moment
like incense of euphoria
grief eventually comes, descends
like on the hills now covered
with snow, so too, the news
blankets the realm, mourned by all
who comprehend
the horrific message
it transcends the letter
like the harsh words
haltingly spoken, remnants of truth
like I turn aside
choosing instead to deny the loss
the passing of the once-brave youth
silence wails quietly, kneels before me
then swallows the air, stagnated
like the days before me
so filled with abject despair
like the resistance of the widow
I hide my veiled face
from truth's debate
I seek a miracle
or at least an answer
as to why the price paid
affords me no peace

Shadows

Staring back on the screen, silent images
Growing old, growing older, becoming wiser
But why solely reserved
For those only who have the key

He remembers their innocence
They are more than what he remembers

Hostility's actions have held hostage
From him his loving family, their history
So, what, from the mystery of life, is he
To make of this predicament

The innocents are blameless
Both those residing near and far

Reliving the joy and anguished days and ways
Memory is the repository for pain's ability
To persevere; yet, it often leaves him smoldering
In impossibility's blame and flame

The innocents and he are weary, saddened
Their shadows, he is unable to explain

An offering, a prayer, that a reunion will come
With apologies, hugs. Thankful and blessed
Is he who has lived to see the hostages
Released, each pardoned by God's grace

Step forward, reveal yourself, cast off
Your shadow, for you have been set free

Downfall

More is better
Is it not?
The taste desired
Be it sweet or hot

Ladders, strong
Or fragile
Climb us to the top
Off we go, we cannot stop

Satisfaction for the moment
Stirs the addictive pot
Nothing is better, is it not?
We, then, buy the entire lot

Falling now atop our heads
All that we have bought
And now we pay the cost
By doing what we ought

Believe It or Not

You've probably heard about old Mr. Pierce. He and his family vanished one day. Mysteriously. Most everyone around here thought it wasn't a big deal that he was gone. That's not nice, but that's part of the story.

Lest you think this a harsh assessment, listen as I tell you something about the tale I heard when I was a little girl, but considerably bigger than a grasshopper, as my grandfather used to say. And, because Grandpa said it, it must be so. My Momma told me the story. She said that Grandpa, her father told it to her. Intended or not, it froze me up until I was filled with fear. She vows it really happened, and today, she still stands by it.

You can believe it or not. So, here's the story.

The Pierces were a poor family. No one seemed to know what old man Pierce did, except that he drank. His reputation was stained much like the squalor in which he, his wife and children lived. They lived up the way, in the holler on the left-hand fork of the road that leads away from the town. City folks would insist we say "hollow," but they don't live around here. Neighbors would laugh if we said *hollow*.

Mountain-folk call things the way we see them. And, if you don't know, a holler is the narrow "V"-shaped space resting between two mountains. Roads in hollers are generally unpaved with potholes that seem to propagate. The puddles, too, when it rains. Critters, both the tame and wild, and the flying kind, feast on the filth, threatening everyone's health. But, when the dry-eyed-sky breathes hot, the road becomes a dust-bowl, combined with coal-dust from nearby coal mines. The word "clean", found only by searching it out in the pages of Webster's Dictionary, under the letter, "c" where one can also find "coal."

The Pierces lived in a three room-house, a "shack" by name given by those who shamed and blamed. The fragile strings of poverty controlled whether the people lived or died. And, coal-miners had Black Lung to deal with.

Father told me that Margaret was a little girl who used to live around here. She would be about my age now. One day, her mother sent her on an errand, two quarters in her pocket. She was to purchase some honey and honey comb from her uncle Al and aunt Luce. The Pink Lady-apples were to be a surprise gift to them. Their favorites.

Margaret had to pass by the Pierces' house. The number of children they had, no one knows. They never attended public school. No private schools around. What education they got or not would come from their mother. A little girl was standing on the Pierces' porch when Margaret walked past their house. A broken-down fence separated the two of them. Margaret waved a greeting. "Hello there. What's your name?" The little girl, slowly descending the steps, walked over near to where Margaret stood. Hesitating, first looking back over her shoulder, she whispered, "I'm Emmy." Never had Margaret seen her before. Blue eyes, brown hair. Almost naked, wearing only underpants.

Emmy, the little girl, smelled like a wet dog. Supposedly, she looked like it, too. As she ventured to where Margaret stood on the other side of the fence, needing more than repairs, Emmy seemed just as curious of Margaret as Margaret was of her. A chained-up mutt lay unmoving beneath the porch. He appeared as emaciated as Emmy. Margaret offered her an apple. And, before the hungry child could say or think to offer her thanks, Emmy devoured the apple right down to the core. Pitiful was the sight. Margaret gave her the entire bagful of apples. Originally intended as a gift for her aunt and uncle. They, unknowing, yet, they would have approved. Margaret was sure it was the right thing to do. And, as in an admonishing voice, shrill in its threat and intention, Emmy's mother yelled. It was said that Emmy, again, furtively looking over her shoulder, responded by running toward her mother's demand. Some of the apples spilled out onto the dusty dirt-yard.

It was a confusing spectacle. A cloud of fear descended

upon Emmy's pale face. The sweet innocence of the previous moment dissipated into one of abject fear and displeasure. Was it because of Margaret? Or the apples?

Rumor has it that Margaret said she'd best be getting along. And so, fleeing to the other side of the road, she continued on her way to her aunt and uncle's. The two quarters, tucked safely away in her apron-pocket.

After purchasing the honey and honeycomb, Margaret moseyed on home. Her aunt and uncle were busy with canning, and Margaret's mother was waiting for the honey. Walking back past the Pierces' house, Margaret is supposed to have said that it looked abandoned. No one has any idea what happened to Margaret or her family. The years passed, as did her aunt and uncle.

I understand from Father that Mrs. Pierce and the children went to Ohio at some point. Supposedly, her brother came to retrieve them. The weeks turned into months, then everyone forgot all about them. No one seemed to care what happened to the Pierces. Seems they didn't have any friends. The Pierce-family were renters. The house was torn down by the owner, and the land, put up for sale.

After the land was surveyed, a young man and his wife purchased it. They live in a trailer on the exact spot where all of this happened. I imagine an account of the tale was in the local newspaper. But I've never seen or read anything about it in all my years. The surveyors found bones in the back yard, where the pig-pen had stood. The bones matched neither those of a pig or those of any animal.

The coroner ruled the bones human. The marks found on them were made by an axe-like instrument.

Jackie Davis Allen

A Treasure

Like the little child
I once was, I sought
Out a treasure-chest

Made of cardboard
It was one, rescued, relieved
From Granny's canning jars

To the top, I filled it
With the all of the little that I
A six-year-old, possessed

And then, I waited, I hoped
And prayed for release, anxious
For the great adventure to begin

Alas! I had no fairy
Godmother, in disguise
Of an angel or otherwise

In the ensuing years, the hunger
I stored in that treasure-chest
Has grown wings

And unfurled, flying high
Dare I seek to fly
Even higher

Dream-Ramblings

A dream, the other night, held me captive
Until, exhausted with struggling
To fulfill the task assigned, I woke up

Tempted to get a pen and jot it down
I resisted, I had no desire to relive
The dream. Besides, I had worked so hard

I needed to go back to sleep
And get some much-needed rest
Imagine if you will, such a dream

In that dream I was given a stack
Of illustrations to peruse
And in a limited time-frame

I had to assign a title to each
As if each of the illustrations
Were to accompany a chapter in a book

It would have been a long book
Page-wise, judging by the amount of effort
I expended examining the art

And giving each a creative title
That flowed along with the written word
Which I had not even read

Nothing more do I remember. Strange
At some later date, I may attempt
To locate the remnants of that dream

Jackie Davis Allen

The Veil Lifted

Had she made a mistake?
Why was the night weeping?
The stage's curtain so velvety black
Why did it cross over the earth's great might
And follow the scent of nature's track
Taking pulse of passion, now deceased?

Did it taste freedom's delight?
Did it relinquish the fight?
Choosing, then, to bathe in peace
Awash in memory
She now tests the waters
Sings lilting melodies

Like gentle falling leaves
Claiming gift of a swelling treasure
She smiles, forgives
Leaves behind the past
Its disharmonious notes
They are but fading memories

A fact once obscured
By so many trees, she lifts now the veil
From her eyes, says goodnight
Smiles in the delight of discovery
Yet, weeps copious tears for the one
Wailing, the one who lives upstairs

No Illusions . . . through the looking glass

The Poet's Seasonal Affective Disorder

The mirror held most all his thoughts
During the day and all through the long nights
The letters held his innermost secrets
By which the accusing Voice did indict

How tightly he did attempt
To hold himself

Against the loose and errant wanderings
Of the disillusioned and littered landscape
By which the shadows
Darkly draped over his life

Like the snowflakes
Falling from the sky

Which painted white the landscape
Of the darkened surface
Below his wingless and mortal psyche
It traced the dark shadows

Troubled as the face of his mind
It mimicked the deep chasm of love lost

The void and emptiness of his heart
Were like the apparition in the mirror
Fading along the edges
And he was losing all sense of time

His mind images, hidden
Trembling, cold, becoming frigid

Jackie Davis Allen

Impossible for any but him to see
The imprint etched such sorrowful and deep lines
Filling his life with lost possibilities
His todays, yesterdays, and tomorrows

Still a source of sunshine, beamed down
A surprising ray of hope, released

From the pages, he began slowly
To reclaim the image of himself
Witness now the sunshine, the open windows
For he, as apparition, no longer exists

Nor does anyone or anything exist
That can exert its power over him

Away with taunts of doom
Poetically speaking, only the Voice
Of his heart speaks for him, the music
Of which has found love's path

Like a song inviting life
His pen moves decisively
Across the pages lying before him
Erasing shadows

The Letter and Its Aftermath

It is such a dark and dreary day
This cold wintery morning, and it is raining
And I am inconsolable
As I face the life ahead of me

I remember the two soldiers outside my door
And how my heart acknowledged the knock, knock
As I anxiously opened it for them

On a blast of rushing wind, my spirit, overwhelmed
For I saw something in their grave and stoic faces
One holding a letter, fastened
With no hope or promise

Alas! Death had come calling
O, Lord, have mercy!

One of them gently said, as he handed me *the, the*
I can hardly bring myself to say it, *the, the letter*

"Here you are, Miss. Do you want us to stay?"

The soldiers stood, refusing to take a seat
And, as they awkwardly waited
I read and wept
Oh, how my heart dropped
Spilling onto the ground!
Terrible words blurred, exploding
What was left of my world

My dear Miss Buchanan
We are most grieved to say
With the heaviest of heart in hand

Jackie Davis Allen

That your dearest one passed away on Friday
Captain John Campbell was a brave young man
And there on the battlefield, he met his end
Awaiting, now, as we all, the Resurrection Day

One of the soldiers cried out:
"Oh, no, you should not be alone!"
And I, stiffly, replied, "I will be all right
Please leave, you must not stay
There is nothing for you to do"
And, then, I distinctly remember, I said
"Go, for I have something I must do"

I watched as they went around the bend
Then closed the door
Oh, Lord, I prayed!
That I could have left with them

I put the letter aside, and told myself
I will attend to these buttons
And with stiffened lips and determined stitches
I began to attach the round reminders
Onto my wedding dress, the one
Handed down by my mother, the one
I would have worn, when we were wed
Had my beloved John come home

The oval frame with his likeness
Now, closeted and buried in the trunk
So handsome, he, in his immaculate uniform
It reminds me of my own battened-down self
Longing, in the anticipation, to be pressed
Down by John's passionate and tender kisses
I am going around in circles today
With no sense of comprehension
I place my arms round about my body
Fortified only by fasteners

No Illusions . . . *through the looking glass*

Oh, Lord, have mercy on me!
What a blow Death has dealt

And still, I wonder how these pearl buttons
Between my breasts can be so cruel
They, which had waited for John's hands

It was he who would have brightened
Even the darkest and dreariest of days
Now, his smile is gone; the weeks have passed
And I sit here with the pearl buttons
Sadly-stitched and helplessly
Clutching at the bodice of my gown

Oh, what ecstasy it would have been
To have had him release them;
To awaken the longing and searing heat
That would have caressed my womanhood!
But, alas! He is no more

Never will my beloved trace his fingers
Around the milky abalone of my breasts
They, which I have long held
Buttoned up and secured, a gift for him
And only for him

Now, the rain has lessened
Only memories descend from on high
I have resigned my worrisome sighs
And keep my mouth and eyes closed
To the truth, fearing it might strike and stain
The silken and satin treasure I am now wearing
The one that would have wed me
To my beloved Captain, John Campbell

But, instead, I stand upright, without a choice
Laced up, waiting for the time, the words
That will forever change my life

Jackie Davis Allen

I am made to cast aside my mourning gown
Of sorrow, though consciously, I am bound
Up in grief, even as, today, I wear
This gown of bridal silk and satin

Oh, it is such a dark and dreary day!
This cold wintery morning
And, it is raining again
And, I am inconsolable
As I face the life
Ahead of me

As in a trance, I walk down the aisle
Resolutely viewing my resignation
Through the veil of stitches
Surrounding the pearls
The ones that march down the front
Of my wedding gown
And the one's which John's brother
Is now claiming as his right
To unloosen

A Portion of Catherine Buchanan's Diary

March 1, 1862

Dawn greets me, and the house seems so cold and empty, creaking at the joints, as I await the warmth of the fireplace to give me strength to keep from retiring back to my bedchamber. I must write out my thoughts, for they are my only comfort during these frightening days.

John has yet to reply to my letter of last month, and I am left wondering how it is that Nate was able to return to their old home place? I have heard he is caring for their ailing mother since her husband's untimely death of February last. O, God! Is there not a way to sufficiently manufacture a way to bring John home safely to me?

A few pansies are poking up their colorful heads from beneath the melting snow. They are more hopeful than I.

Catherine E. Buchanan
Carter County, Tennessee

September 30, 1862

We are running low on candles; so, I will write until I can see no more, or else, I will retire when the worrisome shadows rise up out of the floor. I will, of course, let John read my diary when he returns home from the war. Still, to myself and to you, my silent friend, I give your pages only a little of my sorrow. I should be patient, but I am not.

Catherine

October 1, 1862

Suffering for long, yet, with anticipation, I wait, uneasily, for the day when John will come home, praying safety. Praying that all lingering anxieties and fears will be gone, and John and I, our wedding vows, we will take. O Lord, when will that be? No one seems to know. Too many young bloodied and mangled bodies lie in yonder battlefields and above the scene, the death knell crows.

Why must this senseless rage burn across our land with brother waging war against brother. They, who once grew up loving one another? Sorry that I am to say, that of John and his brother Nate, the one born ten years to the date after the other, both equally convinced of the other's lunacy. One, supporting the Union and the other, supporting the Confederacy. Yet still, they and others do. The north and the south have risen up in debate, the terrible consequences of which falls on our shoulders. Such is our fate . . .

Deprivation within the States is varied and in multitudes. Though, I hesitate to record or enumerate our plenty, out of respect for the indescribable hardships and terrors of our brave soldiers who are experiencing far greater horrors. O, Lord, how much longer must we endure?

Catherine, Carter County, TN

October 11, 1862

I am trying to keep myself occupied lest I turn gray before my time. Daily I pray to God. Is there ever any end to the suffering we must endure? I love you, my dearest John.

Catherine

October 12, 1862

The pigs got loose this morning, and the clothesline must be restrung and all the laundry must be redone . . . Last evening's rain did not help . . .

C.B.

October 17, 1862

I hear such tales, it seems they cannot be true. We, women-folk, are trying to do the best we can. It is hard with no men around to help. I pray the winter will be mild and that our country will not long be divided. Pray to God our States may once again return to some kind of normalcy at war's end. Pray God the war will end soon. I miss John.

Catherine Buchanan

October 23, 1862

The leaves have left the trees, and impregnable upon the ground, they lay frozen, mute in deathly decomposing heaps. Sinking into that final sleep, like our brave heroes of late. My sanity strives, scarcely proper to compose this verse. Tarnished before the world, our future swims in a red sea, drowned. Whose hour, it seems, a promise doomed, shall even worsen. May it not be so. I worry so about John.

Catherine Elizabeth

October 24, 1862

This morning, all is quiet, covered with a cold blanket of purest white. Such a vision. I lament finding any comfort from the sleepless memory of the evening past, filled with echoing, shocking blasts, incompatible within the window of belief, which like my optimism is failing fast.

C. E. Buchanan

Jackie Davis Allen

October 27, 1862

Mamma plans on making a root-stew today, and, two hours past noon, the day of my seventeenth year will be left behind, in care of my muse, a fading image, yet, stamped by the day of my birth. The yellow ribbons John gave me before he left, I will wear in my hair. Were my lover, my beloved soldier, able to join me this afternoon, I would have a reason to smile, and thus, resign to the scarred earth all the tears I have expunged from the heavens in supplicating prayer.

Catherine Elizabeth

October 28, 1862

The children in the neighborhood cling to their mothers' skirts. I fear they have grown old, even as I have, before their time. Nothing seems to smooth their dreams, or their hurts, or mine. Either during the day or at night. It seems such a crime that so many fathers, brothers, cousins and uncles will never return. O, how our hearts yearn to see them once more, whole or in part!

Catherine

November 11, 1862

I have not felt like writing any prose or poetry recently. Sleep has not come often, and seldom has it come easily. I envision the worst, praying it not be so.

Catherine
Carter County, Tennessee

No Illusions . . . *through the looking glass*

July 13, 1864

Dear Diary,

More than a year of memories has passed, when first I heard the news and grief was born. Wild-eyed and distraught, my tears copiously flowed as if from a nightmare's most horrific storm. Yet, none stained the bridal silk and satin in any way, the one in which I was betrothed to have worn on my wedding day to Nate's brother John. For, you see, my beloved Captain John Campbell became a statistic on that terrible Friday.

Grief, so heavy, descended upon me that I have not felt like putting into words the sorrow that has engulfed me over his tragic loss, and yes, I might add, my loss as well.

Shock, duty to tradition led me to acquiesce and to perform as I became the wife of Nathan Campbell. He is the brother of my dearly beloved Captain John Campbell who died at Vicksburg, Mississippi, on July 13, 1863.

As sorrow reigned over my grief-stained mourning-needs, dark clouds ushered me into a matrimonial estate with Nathan, called Nate. Even before my lover's memorial flowers had a chance to go to seed, we were wed.

It was in the war, the most uncivil war, the War between the States where John, my dearest one, fell to his knees in final fatality. Nate would be most-distressed if he should come across my diary, but he has nothing to fear. For, in this past year, I have come to love him dearly.

A part of me still aches, buried with John's fate; his remains, never recovered. Or, if they were, no letter has come to let me know. In truth, my aching heart never had a chance to heal before I was found kneeling in submission at the altar, an alarming tradition, with John's dear brother.

How is it, that of the fairer sex, that unjustly, I am considered property? I realize it is not as if I am an exception. For, as I have heard of late, many of my women friends have suffered the same cruel fate.

When will this merciless war be over?

Catherine Buchanan Campbell

Despite Improbability's Call

Within lay-tools, implements
Innocent of her design, her intent
If successful
If she changed her errant ways
If prayers could fly
If she had wings
Destiny and fortune
Would befriend her
Long-held dream

From pattern of inspiration
She chose to place herself
On the other side of fate
Who had made it her business
To interfere in her life
Claiming that the wanderlust
Flowing through her veins
Was to blame
Giving no never-mind

To naysayers, nature's child
With renewed resolve
With each and every misstep
Inside the black hole
Of wanting and needing, she
Dreamed dreams that blossomed
Like bright-shining stars, and despite
Improbability's echo, she reached out
And created a star of her own design

Jackie Davis Allen

Treasured Memories

Grandma was sitting on the green glider on the front porch of her house, high up in the mountains of southwestern Virginia. Her feet were planted on the wooden porch, her body moving back and forth, back and forth, as was the glider. Sluggish flies congregated onto sticky yellow tapes hanging from the sky-blue bead board-ceiling.

The Saturday Evening Post lay by Grandma's side, the well-worn pages, flat as the air was still, hot and sticky-sweet. On the hillside adjacent to their yard, stands a Paw Paw-tree. With their yellow innards exposed, the paw paws lay where they'd fallen while the summer-sun stressed their sweet fruit into a hot gooey mess. The yellow jackets swarmed over the rotting mass, and I knew well to stay away, lest I get stung by those dreaded flying insects.

Standing next to the hand pump, a fair distance away from the yellow jackets and their yellow feast, I pumped and pumped, managing to coax out some wet coolness. It spilled out over my bare feet. With my cupped hands, I splashed some on my face and drank until I was filled. Grandma continued to sit on the porch, the glider and she moving, back and forth. I went back to sit beside her, noticing that she'd rolled down her stockings which were now resting down around her ankles, the elastic garters caught up in rolls.

Grandma looked ancient and tired. She was tall and soft-spoken. And because of the heat, neither of us had the energy to talk; so, we just sat there. I watched with curiosity as she slowly braided her long white hair, which she'd just washed with the shampoo whose commercial rang out over the radio's air waves: "Halo, Everybody, Halo. Halo is the shampoo that glorifies your hair, so . . ." Everyone knew the jingle. Grandma didn't understand why her once-black hair, turned white long ago, was suddenly turning yellow. Later, she was to discover the shampoo had dye coloring in it. She never used "Halo" again.

Except for her clothing and the pictures in library

books, I thought that Grandma could have been a queen. Dressed in an attractive printed and colorful feed-sack dress that my mother had made for her, and with an apron tied around her waist, she sat regally on her glider-throne. With up-lifted arms, she wound the long snaking braid around the back of her head. She brought one hand up to her lips and then back to her head, and inserted a Bobby pin. One by one, the pins traveled from her aproned lap, to her hand, then to her mouth, and finally, the pins rested, snuggled inside the braid. An ancient crown of might.

 I went back to the hand-pump. It was difficult to pump, but finally, once again, cool water sprang forth. My bare feet delighted in the trickles that splashed between my toes. I bent over, gulped down a swallow, and continued to pump. Up and down. Up and down. As the sweat ran down my face and arms, I noticed that the water had already evaporated in the area surrounding my feet. It was hot. Grandma beckoned me to rejoin her. The mud between my toes had turned to dust. I wiped my feet on the rag that served as a mat, and sat back down near my grandmother. We sat, not too close together, moving back and forth, on the pale-green glider. It was a lazy kind of day.

 It was too hot to do much of anything. It is a special treat for me to be sitting with my grandmother. "Sitting" is a treat for my grandmother, especially, since she has to work so hard in the kitchen-garden, and up in the fields. The fields were where the orchard and canning gardens were. She had Grandpa, the chickens and the hog to take care of, too. Maybe she was resting her heart. Momma always told me to be real good when I was at Grandma's because she had heart-trouble. Momma would usually say, something like, "Don't aggravate your grandmother." Wiping sweat off her forehead, with the back of her arm, Grandma turned to me and asked, "Sweetie, would you like some Kool-Aid?" I really liked lemonade better, but I knew that lemons cost money. I remembered my manners and answered, "Yes, thank you, Grandma."

 Grandma slipped her shoes back on and stood up,

slowly smoothing out her apron. I could just guess what she was going to say next. And, I wasn't wrong. "Honey, you stay out here; I'll bring yours out to you." Momma always reminded me, "Now, don't you be upsetting or pestering your grandmother." I wasn't aware that there were different kinds of heart problems and since we never talked about it, Grandma and me, or Momma and me, I just tried to be a good little girl. I didn't want to cause her to have a heart attack. So, I just kept quiet. Grandma returned with the Kool-Aid, and we sat there sipping the cold drinks and with me watching how the ice seemed to disappear. Grandma's feet had to be hurting because the glider slowed down. I just watched the bees nibbling on the paw paws.

    Nothing much was moving. Of course, the yellow sticky fly-tape had evidence that the flies were not lazy. There were no coal trucks rumbling down the road. The railroad tracks were silent; at least they would be for a little while. The steam engine-powered-locomotive that roared down the tracks on the other side of the mountain was much more formidable than my mother was. When I sneaked out to play in my grandparent's fields high up in the mountains, I knew what to expect. A whipping. Or, a switching. However, that coal black monster train, no one ever knew when it was going to stop, for how long or when it would start back up again. I thought, what if I ever got trapped on the other side of the mountain, and not be able to get across the tracks to go home? That was a scary thought. And, it was one thing I was not willing to risk. So, I never ever sneaked across the road, across the creek or across the railroad tracks to visit my great aunt Rosie. Except once, and I never made it to her house.

But, that's another story.

Grandma finally broke the silence. "You know my sister, Bet, don't you?"

"Yes, Grandma, she and Uncle live up the road. Her son, and

uncle Stew, your youngest son, are real good friends."

"Yes. Let me tell you a story about your Aunt Bet."

Grandma thus began: "She doesn't like to be stuck at the house all of the time. So, one day, she asked her husband to get her a Jeep. She told him she wanted to learn to drive. Well, she was nigh on to being well past sixty when he got her that Jeep. She told me she wanted a vehicle that was open. That way, she figured, she'd be able to jump out if she got into a pickle and did not know what to do, like forgetting how to stop it."

Grandma continued, "That's exactly what happened. She got to going too fast and forgot how to stop the Jeep. She put her foot on the clutch instead of the brake. She was thrown out, and that's how she broke her leg."

Grandma's sister was just about as ancient as she was. In fact, she was only a year or so older than Grandma. Both, she and Grandma had long white hair. I didn't know whether aunt Bet ever used "Halo" shampoo or not, but I don't remember seeing any yellow in her hair.

I'd never ever heard either my grandmother or my grandfather express a desire to drive. Of course, they couldn't afford to buy a car. That might have been why. Whenever they needed to go somewhere, they rode on the county bus like we did. However, once Poppa managed to buy a car, a Hudson, he'd offer to take them over to town. As a matter of fact, I didn't know of any old people who drove a vehicle. Except, now, I knew at least one did. Or had, until she broke her leg. Aunt Bet was more courageous than I could've imagined.

The mountainous roads had early on persuaded me to yield to my fears, and, always, I rode over to the county seat sitting in the floor of the back seat of my Poppa's old black car, the Hudson. I didn't like looking out the window to down below where the car might tumble over the mountain. I worried that the coal trucks might take over our side of the road and we would fall off the side of the mountain down, into the deep gully below. I'd heard tales about just that kind of thing happening. I prayed that God would take care of me and let me get to town and back home safely.

I was young and little, but I just knew that God had something special in store for me. He obviously had answered my prayers. Otherwise, I would have died long ago and I wouldn't be telling you this story. Aunt Bet must have been braver than her sister. Grandma interrupted my thoughts. "I've got to get back to work now, but I'll walk you home." After rinsing our Kool-Aid glasses, my grandmother set our drinking glasses, really, they were jelly jars, on the wooden cart. That cart was the one that sat next to one of the front doors, the door that led to the living room, the door where the pots of geraniums and begonias sat on either side. She turned the glasses upside down to keep out the flies.

We stepped off the porch onto the dusty yard, where even the chickens were too lazy to come and eat the corn. I'd earlier shelled it off the cob. I tossed it out and up into the air, calling to them, "Here, chick, chick, chick". I was hoping to entertain myself as they scattered here and yon looking for their favorite delicacy. I wondered if they were sleeping. Even Grandma's orange lilies, "flags", as she called them, drooped their heads and leaned over as if they'd not the strength to stand. As we walked down the hill, stepping on the large flat stones that served as steps, the flags, planted on either side of the steps, brushed my right arm. Something yellow had stuck to my arms.

"That's pollen." I squinted, from the yellow brightness and the tears mingled with the sweat on my face. Grandma wiped my eyes with her apron strings. We'd not yet reached the road. "Grandma, why are tears coming out of my eyes?" "It's the pollen that's causing it, sweetie. It's the same thing that causes your throat to feel sore and why you have trouble breathing." I was too exhausted to ask any more questions. We walked along the narrow country road toward my house, just two houses away, counting hers and another.

The hot tar oozed up from the pavement, making bubbles. I wiped my forehead with the back of my arm as my grandmother lifted the hem of her apron and wiped her glasses. I tried to avoid the tar and, sometimes, was able to walk in the dust that'd accumulated alongside the road. My bare feet ached and I could hardly wait to get home. As we passed Aunt Rosa's garden, the milkweed wings were asleep. The plants were all bunched up against the aged and darkened split-rail-fence.

"The seeds will eventually float through the air and the Monarch butterflies will have to find another place to feast, or maybe, they'll migrate like the birds at the end of the summer."

That's what my Poppa said when I asked him about the birds that filled the sky at the end of the summer.

"They're going south for the winter."

So, maybe that's where the butterflies would go too.

Anyway, there was no wind, and the milkweed wings just lazily stayed put. All I wanted to do was to get home, suck on an ice cube, and put my feet in a pan of cool water.

"Momma, come on in."

Grandma and I climbed the steps to our house where my own Momma was waiting.

"I just made a pitcher of ice water."

Grandma and Momma sat down at the kitchen table, and I went out onto the back porch to get a pan so I could soak my bare feet. I hoped they weren't blistered from the tar. I slowly lowered the water bucket down into the hand-dug well. I pulled the rope against the pulley with all of my might. The braided rope hurt my hands. I was afraid that the bucket's weight would pull me back into the well. The rope made my hands ache even more. Finally, I had the bucket up against the side of the well. Whew! I reached over with one hand, while still holding onto the rope, and never mind that the bucket tilted and half of it spilled all over me! I smiled happily with delight as the cold water soaked into my clothes, cooling off my body.

Suddenly, dark clouds began to shade the sun, and it seemed as if night had come early. The loud thunderous roars that echoed were neither coming from the Norfolk and Western locomotive across the way nor from the ferocious coal trucks that so often went by our house every workday. It was beginning to rain! I put the water bucket aside, so as not to touch the metal, for I knew that lightening might soon come and I did not want to get a shock. Ah! My feet rejoiced as they soaked in the basin of water.

One time, I'd touched the electric stove and the sink at the same time and goose pimples rose upon my back and all over and even onto my scalp. And, they did not go away and they hurt awfully. Momma smeared Vick Salve all over me, bundled me up into a blanket, tight as a straight-jacket, and put me to bed. I didn't know which was worse, the shocking experience or not being able to get out of the blanket roll! Somehow, the home-remedy worked. When I woke up, the goose pimples were all gone.

"Well, I guess I'd better be going."

Grandma kissed my forehead. She and Momma walked back into the living room on the way to the front porch. The wind began to whip up, the trees were swaying; the temperature, falling.

"It's about time that it rained. Or else, my garden would have just up and died. Thank the Good Lord for the rain!"

Grandma sounded happier than she'd at any other time during that week. I don't know what she and my mother talked about while I'd been out back. Maybe the weather?

No Illusions . . . *through the looking glass*

I've forgotten whether or not I'd sneaked out to my grandparents' house or whether or not Momma'd asked Grandma to take me off her hands! I always seemed to get into trouble and get the most whippings. If I'd sneaked out to my grandmother's house, surely, I'd have remembered it because my mother always followed through on everything, especially punishment for disobedience. And "sneaking" of any kind was disobedience in my mother's book. I didn't get a whipping, so I guess, Momma must have been in a good mood to let me go out to visit her mother.

From where I was standing on our front porch, I could see Grandma climbing up the hill to her house just as the rain really began to come down. It was beginning to get cold. And the rain was beginning to blow in onto the porch although the porch had a roof over it. Our porch-swing began to move back and forth all by itself, but really, it was the wind that was moving it. Looking out the window of our front door, I saw the many pink-flowered trees in the middle of the yard looking sad. All branches and flowers of the Mimosa Tree drooped. The pink blossoms appeared to be crying. Strangers used to stop alongside the road and get out and ask if they could take a picture of our tree. They were so impressed with the fluffy pink flowers. But that didn't last long because Poppa couldn't stand the mushy mess they made in the yard when they fell. The yellow jackets liked them and there was too much danger for us children to get stung.

During the summer, our house was always cooler than my grandparent's house. Their house sat upon a hill, not far from where we lived. Our air-conditioning was the natural non-mechanical kind. Our house was cooler, my father said, because it had something to do with our house being so close to the side of the mountain. Momma called out, "Get ready for supper."

Well, she did not have to issue that invitation twice. The temperature had dropped so much it was almost cold. Momma'd heated up the pinto beans she'd taken out of the refrigerator. She'd cooked them yesterday in her pressure cooker. She'd selected some tomatoes, which she'd picked earlier. They came from the bushel basket sitting on the covered back porch. Then, she switched on the oven-light and checked the corn bread. It was almost ready. The warm kitchen odors reached my nose. Supper was ready. Momma said, "Sissy, get a knife and slice the tomatoes."

My oldest sister always got to help with the cooking. I suppose the one time that my mother went out to the garden on the side of the hill to work and left me sitting on a stool to watch the beans was the reason. I'd just sat there and watched them. Watch them burn! I'd tried to explain. No one told me to do anything but watch them. And that was exactly what I did. I still remember that awful smell.

Momma made my favorite wilted-lettuce salad. If you've never had it, you can't possibly know what you've missed! Mind you, I've never made it, but I've watched my mother. She fried some bacon. After removing the bacon, she set it out to drain and to get crisp. Then, she mixed some vinegar into the hot bacon grease. I loved to hear that sizzling sound! She poured it over the torn lettuce leaves and chopped green onions. Sprinkling it with a little salt, she then crumbled the bacon over top of it. So yummy!

The table was set with a water glass here, a jelly jar there. A fork and knife here, and a spoon there. Those odd and assorted implements were our everyday and Sunday best. With Momma's corn bread, pinto beans, wilted-lettuce salad and sliced tomatoes, what more could anyone have wanted? Perhaps, a glass of lemonade?

By the time supper was over, the sun had come back out and the rain had gone away. Almost as if by magic, the air was once again warm. After my sisters and I washed the dishes and put them away, Momma went into her bedroom and brought out her black crocheted pocket book. It was the one that Aunt Lot had made. I remember how bumpy it felt when I stroked it. Momma'd always carried it with her when she went to the post office to mail the money orders to pay the electricity bill, and the bills for B & L May-Tag, the Lester's, and Poppa's insurance. She fumbled around and found what she was looking for.

"Sweetie, here's some change. I want you to go up to the store and get something for Aunt Bet. Watch out for the trucks and cars, and go up and keep her company. She's home from the hospital, and it'd be nice if you visited her."

The rain had left puddles on the road. It was no longer dark as night. The summer rainstorm had come and gone. I was a little afraid. I did know where the store was. But going by myself was a little scary, as I'd never done it before. The stick-built and unpainted store, darkened with age, was up the road, around the curve, and just a little piece above that. For some reason, there were few vehicles on the road that day. I dodged the puddles along the way, though I'd wanted to splash in them. What fun that would have been! Could it have been Sunday?

    Anyway, I found the store. It was just where I thought it was. It sat right smack dab between Mamie and Thea's houses. Mamie and Thea were sisters, and since Thea had no children, and Mamie had two sons and a daughter, she gave her daughter to Thea. I'd never heard such a thing in my entire life. I'd also heard that each of Mamie's children had a different father. But I didn't know if that had anything to do with her decision to give up her daughter. I'd heard that Mamie ordered her husbands from a mail order-catalogue, though the only catalogues I was familiar with were Sears Roebuck, Montgomery Ward and Alden's. Those were the ones that Grandpa called the "Wish Books". Often, he'd let us order something, always saying, "Charge it to me." Grandpa was more generous than Grandma.

    I finally reached the store, about a mile up the road from my house. I walked up the two steps, onto the porch where old men sat on nail kegs and chairs. They were chewing tobacco, smoking cigarettes and dipping snuff. Tin cans sat next to three wooden chairs with woven seats, tilted back onto two legs. Plop! Plop-Ping. One stream of tobacco juice missed the can. The bearded one hit the target. The white-haired man with the slouched hat, pulled down, almost over his eyes, had spat, and his spit hit the metal can. The ringing sound conveyed his success. The old men talked softly amongst themselves, as they reminisced over the old days of working for the lumberyard or the coal-mines.

I wondered if they talked about the "War", something that adults stopped talking about when they sensed I was nearby? Encased in overalls, their exposed and sweat-kissed skin glistened in the sun. Steam traveled upwards from the porch as the temperature increased. I wanted to enter the store, though I was a bit afraid. Walking into that darkened space, shaking my head, as if that would help me regain my sight, I tried to adjust from the outside to the inside. I saw that the winter's potbellied stove was still there, sitting center-stage. Encircling the silent stove, five or six old men sat, perched on nail kegs. Were they remembering their youth and days gone-by?

I gave the storekeeper my change and told him, my finger on the glass showcase window, "I want that one."

"That one" was those little candy hearts. They must have been left over from Valentine's Day. The storekeeper handed me the bag. I was so proud of myself. I still had about a half mile to go. And, those candies were so tempting! However, I resisted the temptation, for I knew they were for my great aunt. I tried to think of what I would say to Aunt Bet. Though she was really my great aunt, I called all of my Grandma's sisters *aunt*. Most of the time, when I was with adults, I had to listen to them. However, sometimes I'd want to say something too. But I was always told I had to wait until the grownups were finished. By the time they'd finished, I couldn't remember what I'd wanted to say. Then, when I'd get a chance, like this morning with Grandma, I couldn't think of anything at all to say.

With the bag of candies grasped tightly in my hand, I walked out of the store, down the porch steps. Carefully crossing the road, I continued on my journey. I could see Aunt Bet's house in the distance, up on the hill, on the left side of the road. I was nearly there. I walked across the footbridge, and glanced down at the creek. As I climbed up the long driveway, unpaved with the tire ruts filled with pools of water, I thought that must have been where she'd the accident. The bag had begun to wilt. My hands were sweating. The top part of the paper bag, containing the candy, was as limp as a dishrag. I finally reached the steps leading up to Aunt Bet's house. She was sitting there in her rocking chair with one leg propped up, the one with the cast.

"Come on up", she said.

"Hi, Aunt Bet." I handed her the bag. "These are for you."

She looked into the bag. "Why don't you just keep them? Here, go ahead!"

She smiled at me, and since she'd given me permission, I gladly accepted them and sat back down on a chair, about six feet away from her, the door to the house between us.

"Come here and sign my cast!"

She invited me to come closer. I carefully wrote my name.

"Would you like a glass of apple cider?"

"No, thank you."

I'd never had apple cider. I just knew it had alcohol in it. Poppa'd once tried to make something with apples. When Momma found the smelly liquid, sitting on the hillside in one of her pots, she took off the rock, which held the lid down. The smell of the liquid told her it had fermented. It had alcohol in it! Well, now, since my mother was a tee-totaler, that meant my father had to be too. But he wasn't.

So, torn between being thirsty and accepting a forbidden drink from an aunt who jumped out of a Jeep, I guessed I'd just have to go thirsty. It wasn't polite to ask for things.

"You must be thirsty. How about a glass of lemonade?"

"Yes, thank you," I politely answered.

We walked into the kitchen, she with her crutches, and I holding the door open for her. I was very much on edge. For her dog had a new litter of puppies, which had been nipping at my ankles. They tried to come inside, which Aunt Bet didn't want. They were nipping at my ankles again. We carried our glasses back out onto the porch, and I handed Aunt Bet her glass and helped put her crutches to the side of her rocking chair. The puppies kept nipping at my ankles, and I kept silent as I sat on the porch-glider, opposite aunt Bet and her rocking chair. I scraped my ankles with first one shoe and then the other, trying to stop the puppies from nipping at my ankles. It didn't work, not one little bit. Truth be told, I was afraid of them. I couldn't concentrate on much of anything. I was hot and tired from walking in the steamy heat. The puppies had exhausted me for I'd no experience with puppies.

    Momma always tooted the horn when she went anywhere. She'd a reputation for needing guided assistance from her car to anyone's house to make sure that their dog would not bite. Most dogs are not biters, I later discovered. However, those little critters, the puppies, have scratchy paws. Aunt Bet, must have gotten tired from trying to elicit some conversation from me, because she thanked me for coming. With that, I said goodbye, knowing that I still had some left-over candy to share. I also had the makings for a good bedtime story for my little sister.

Wandering

The entrance to the building
Is surrounded by guards
So too, the exits, but I have managed
To flee the grounds. I have found a way
And am now the person I was intended to be

I am intent upon my work
And I am painting, creating
A moment in time, surreal

And the image I am painting is framed
By illusion's fertile imagination
Not a moment is there to waste
A smile beams upon my face
It is an unlikely scene

So too, for me to be painting a canvas
This early in the morning, for
In the distance, on the shore

I see a young girl
She is three or four or so
And she is playing with a little boy
Like the day, their promise holds much joy
Oh! She is running. A trailing string

In her little hands; it is escaping
She is struggling, and the little boy is falling
And the kite's beribboned tail is crying

In this cold and windy morning
Alas! The wind is mourning
And I am trying to keep from wailing

Jackie Davis Allen

I am wondering, if in the painting
What it is that is happening, is actually
Happening to the little girl and boy

The uniform of the guard spells danger
And his firm grasp on my arm
Knocks my paints to the ground
"For your own good", he says

As he leads me to the place
Where I am inside my room
Wandering, searching for the how
To reconcile my abandonment

The Timepiece

His clock ticks throughout the night
Beneath a heavy blanket of concern
His sorrow and he, both, misunderstood
He is praying for relief, for understanding

The floorboards groan until he falls asleep

He is but one of the sojourners in this world
Gifted with an inquisitive nature and blessed
With creativity and opportunity
Hesitation is his long-time enemy

And still, he longs for recognition

O, gift of insight, friend of fresh dawn
Will you not gather him unto you?
Go now with your enigmatic smile!
Go with sweet kisses of morning's delight!

Go before the day grows old!

Jackie Davis Allen

The Door

The door, behind which I stood
Was locked, though I could see him
Through the peep-hole
He was standing out there, holding
His hat in his weathered hands
I could discern no smile
As he knocked, I took pity
On the night's ghastly apparition
Neither did he enter nor did he leave
When I opened the door
I bade him welcome
Told him to come on in
He just stood there
Silent, mute
Or, did I imagine that?
The night was dark and eerie
It gave me such a fright
And then, despite chilling me
To the depths
Of my being
The candle . . . it flickered
It shook the cobwebs
Out of my most troubled head
An account of all of this
Was in the morning papers
And as I read, I wondered
Ought I not try to find
Other ways of exorcising
What is inside my poetic head?

Inside the Aria

And, coming into his arms
Her lover groans and sighs
With passion's ecstasy
With sweetest indulgent cries

And yielding
To intensity's heat
They rise, passionately
Slowly, then quickly

With little regard
To discordant notes
Of the recent past
Like ivory keys

That often sing
Off key, erratically
Yet, within the keep
Inside the aria

They share continuously
A love beyond compare
One that never needs to sleep
A love that never needs to sleep

Jackie Davis Allen

Adolescence

Eruptions have ruined my day
And salty waters flood the rivers
Of my discontent
And torrential rains stream
Down my face, though I search
For a hiding place, I remain
In a constant state of anxiety
I lie around all day and mope and pray
That these disruptive eruptions will go away
To my lament, social media now substitutes
For friends, and in my haste, I decide
To never again show my face

I have suffered long enough
And really do not need
This notoriety

My face crops up everywhere
To my dismay
It is all getting so out of hand
I delete my social media accounts
In an attempt to regain my composure
And those so-called friends, still by my side
Can now stop offering me their opinions
And, finally, lest I lead you astray
I must let you know, I cannot understand
Why the face in the mirror
Looking back at me is so miserable
I told her that her breakouts
Are far less serious than mine

Child of Angst

As far as things go, the young girl of the mountains was glad she lived where she did.

The Child was standing on the front porch, looking across the road, across the creek, and across the railroad tracks to where her great aunt's house stood. There, in the distance, she could barely make out the two chairs tilted back up against the wall, and a swing. Though they looked like little specks, she knew what the specks were. She had visited her great aunt a couple of times. Only one, about which she remembered details. She had climbed the steps to the porch, passing by the porch furniture, and had gone inside. There, to her surprise, she discovered the walls were papered with pages from magazines, newspapers. That was most unlike her own home where the walls were adorned with store bought-wallpaper, changed every couple of years.

The Child's house was underpinned by cement blocks. The cement blocks were there, not because it was on a hill, but just in case the creek flooded. That way, the water would stay down cellar. At least, that was what she had heard in her mother's prayers whenever it rained. Everyone had an outhouse, some had one-seaters and others had two-seaters, and if they were lucky, the Sears Roebuck and Montgomery Ward catalogues would hold out until they could locate another catalogue.

The Child was fond of saying that, if she had had a strong pitching arm, she could have thrown a baseball across the way and hit the side of the mountain where her aunt's house stood. Auntie's house was as dark as the coal that moseyed on down the railroad tracks, piled high in the N & W cars. The Child faintly remembered it having once been whitewashed. The house, that is. But there was little visible evidence of that now.

The Child lived with her parents and four sisters and a brother in a four room-house, painted white, with a tin roof. It was tucked back into the Cumberland Mountains of

Appalachia, where her father, who had served in North Africa back in WWII, had hired his brother-in-law and some neighbors to build the house. Nearby, lived The Child's grandparents, they, who had given her parents the land as a wedding gift. The land was the insurance that ensured we would be living next door to my grandparents. It was the same for her aunts and uncles. The house cost $5000, a steep amount of money to come from her father's coal miner's salary. Saving up that amount of money would have been nearly impossible. So, her father used up all of the money he had received when he was discharged from the army.

  The Child also lived in her mind. She, collecting bits and pieces of information, sights, sounds and imaginations, storing them up for the day when she might need them. Though forbidden to do so, she loved to roam in the mountains where she swung off ancient vines until they broke. And there, where she cupped her hands and drank of the clear mountain stream-water. There, where she explored caves, imagining Cherokee Indians taking refuge from rainstorms and who knows what else.

  Time spent in her grandfather's mountains provided her with the fresh air of freedom from the boredom that chained her to her mother and the chores that were expected of her. She loved the mountains, stealing off to them to experience the freedom that only they could provide. There, she found a measure of peace and solace, even as she realized and accepted the punishment which awaited her return. The cost for her defiance was paid by the relief of boredom and the ensuing demands of her stay-at home-mother. Paradoxically, she disliked the mountains, for she felt confined by them. There were sights and sounds, experiences and adventures to be had beyond the mountains. And so, here, too, she collected her thoughts, tucking them back into her mind. She was determined that, one day, she would leave the mountains behind.

  Often, she wondered by what set of circumstances it was that she and her family lived where they did. She imagined that, a cataclysmic flood, of Biblical proportions had raged through the tall mountains long ago, carving out just enough space to leave the mountains split, forming other mountains. Farther below, was what remained of a creek. If one could call it that, for it was but a memory of the clear waters where The Child had once seen fish leaping for joy. It was filled with the silt of coal now, black with stagnated death. Nearby, on the largest single piece of coveted flat land, lay her great aunt's summer-garden, filled with the finest of sweet potatoes and melons. It snaked alongside the creek and on the other side of the garden, a narrow, winding road served as the transportation route. For coal trucks, coming and going, loaded and unloaded, all day long. That is, until the mines played out. And, it was on this other side of the road, backed up against the base of the split into mountain, where The Child lived. Where she pondered and deliberated on how to make life interesting with the only resources possessed: Her imagination and creativity.

    Given there are no documents to prove this, The Child filed all this back into her mind. She collected bits and pieces of things, storing them up, never knowing when she might need them. And, she knew for certain, one day, she would need them.

    Whatever catastrophic event that had carved out the land where she and her relatives lived, it had left the other side of the mountain with several "V"-shaped wedge-like spaces between it and another mountain. These were called "hollers" in the mountain vernacular. There, houses stood on stilts to prop them up against the side of the mountain.

    It was as if the land she called home, was a way-fare for coal trucks hauling coal one way and returning to pick up another load, and the trains doing the same. Repeating the route of their efforts, over and over. Decade after decade. Generation after generation. The meandering railroad-tracks carried coal cars, filled or empty, and with but only an occasionally and infrequent passenger car. Both, the train and the coal trucks, each winding their way through the mountains, up and down the mountain, around the curvaceous mountain, had but one way in and one way out.

Like a spout, like a funnel, her hopes and dreams were filled with stumbling blocks, little poured forth; she, holding it within, along with her imagination. It would be several years before it was recognized that she needed glasses. And, then, it was as if she was seeing everything as through a magnifying lens. Everything seemed larger than it might have, especially, if it involved her. Even her relationship with her mother. She, placed under such scrutiny, it was as if she had her nose lowered down to discern exactly what it was, she was seeing. And, seeing was part of her perceiving.

"Your daddy might get laid off. If that happens, we'll have to move to where ever he can find work."

For The Child, it was as if the long-awaited script for a movie had handed her its stamp of approval. All that was needed was to "get the show on the road," so to speak. In her imagination, she saw adventure. Never mind that all she could envision were like those images she had seen in her first-grade pre-primer readers. She would be able to ride a bicycle down the sidewalk, fly a kite, and who knows what else. Glory be, the promised land awaited.

There would be sidewalks where things were clean, not covered with the stain of coal. There, where fathers wore suits and carried briefcases. For whatever purpose. And then, perhaps, her mother could wear high heels and fancy aprons and live in a house, landscaped on flat land with flowers and trees, manicured . . . she had heard that word once, and looking down at her bitten and chewed off fingernails, she determined that she would have one of those, too. And, with red fingernail polish.

The Child wondered how she was ever going to make it through the rest of the year. Her best friend, Judy, had given her the bad news.

"Today's my last day. Dad got a job over in West Virginia, and we're moving this weekend."

Judy handed her the note, checking to see if Mr. Jackson was watching. He wasn't.

The Child's heart swelled from pain. She felt like she was about to suffocate. She felt the tears welling up. She tried to stifle a sob, unsuccessfully. Judy was the only friend she had in the eighth grade. Since the county had closed all of the one room-schools, her eighth grade had swollen to the point where, her high school, the only one on this side of the mountain, now had three rooms full of eighth graders. The first time in the school's history. Most of the friends she'd gone to school with since first grade were in the other two classrooms.

"I don't know what I'm going to do. I won't have anyone to talk to. What am I going to do?"

Judy placed her hand on her friend's shoulder and patted it, unable to say anything helpful.

Mr. Jackson was a terror as a geography teacher, but he was quite lenient when it came to study hall. She didn't want to try his patience. If there were to be any repercussions to their passing notes, then The Child would be the one left to suffer, hour upon hour, in the dreaded detention hall.

The two girls sat, one behind the other, their desks pushed up against the wall, adjacent to a long stretch of unused chalkboards, and mostly out of the sight of Mr. Jackson, the young geography teacher. He was partly responsible for the condition of The Child's bitten down-to-the-quick fingernails.

Judy did her best to console her friend, but there was not much she could do or say. Besides, it was difficult to not attract attention. Even if they whispered, as they were doing now. But she didn't feel all that comfortable having to turn around in her desk to face Judy. The Child didn't want any demerits to affect her nearly-perfect report card. For each "A", on every one of her six weeks-report cards, her father gave her a hard-earned silver dime.

Everything seemed turned upside down now that she was in eighth grade. Things had been so much easier when she was in seventh grade. That is, except from having to watch out for Tommy. He, always, waiting at the bus stop to chase her all the way to her classroom. Sometimes, he even managed to hug and kiss her. Ugh! At least, he wasn't in any of her classes this year!

Judy, her very best and only friend, would not be back at school, come Monday. That was that. Only, "that was that" didn't account for all the days she'd be missing Judy with no one to take her place. Whatever was she to do?

Too bad her diary didn't have a lock on it. Besides, it only had space for three lines a day. No one could say what they wanted to say in just three lines. So boring, the same old, like, *went to school today. It rained. Test tomorrow.* Or some such mundane comment. Anything she might otherwise have written would have added fuel to the fire to her embarrassment. Especially, if any of her sisters got a hold of diary and read her most private, personal information. She'd just die.

The Child felt as if she was in a locked box and the key had been thrown away. The box seemed to get smaller and smaller and more oppressive with each day. Funny, she used those words to describe how she felt, especially, since boxes were difficult to come by. The only box she'd seen recently was down in the cellar of her grandparents' house. It held canning jars, spiders, and mouse droppings. Ugh!

The Child held a strange fascination for boxes. One could put so much in them, things like her test papers with the "A's" on them, and the Bible Correspondence tests that had awarded her a free week at a camp in Kentucky. If she'd had a box, the size that she could have pushed under her bed, she could have stashed away that fake fur-wrap that somehow disappeared from the house after she'd worn it to school. Her mother was not concerned that it was missing. Sharing one chest of drawers with her sisters, and it with only three drawers, was not satisfactory.

The Child had no recourse but to get through the rest of the day as best she could. She was a good student, and in spite of her sorrow, she managed to listen and participate in class. That's how she learned best. By listening, and by studying the questions most of the teachers wrote on the board, the ones they had to copy down in notebooks. When it came time to go to the library, she was sadder than ever. Judy's parents had received permission to pick her up early. No chance to have a proper goodbye.

The hall monitors kept little *Teacher's Pet*-pads filled with names of anyone who did anything other than walk softly, making no noise whatsoever. So much to worry about. Miss Carson, the librarian was kinder. Had Judy been able to stay a bit longer, they would have had a chance to sit and whisper and commiserate with one another. Judy was just as sad, for she was going off to a school where she knew no one. At least, during recess, The Child might see some of her classmates from primary years, since all of the eighth graders had the same schedule.

The bell rang, and off to the library, The Child went. She checked out three of the thickest books she could find, paying no attention to the titles. Or, the authors. During the weekend, when she could sneak some time away from her chores, she would seek solace inside the pages. Perhaps, she could forget how miserable she was.

Soon, the closing-bell rang. The Child fled, walking down the long-darkened hall, the oiled hardwood floor-smelling rank, with a mixture of sawdust scattered here and there. Once she had gone through the double doors, and down the steps, she took off running. One could never be sure whether or not the school bus driver would park in the same place. He might even leave early. Leaving her stranded and having to walk home as it had done far too frequently before.

"Honey, cheer up, life has to go on. You'll make some new friends, bye and bye," The Child's mother responded, when she complained.

"It isn't fair. I don't have a friend anymore."

And, with that, The Child, buried her nose in one of her books, and placed even more distance between her mother and herself. You see, the only time The Child saw anyone her age was when she was at school. Even there, she had little time to cultivate friendships.

The school bus came by her house around a quarter to nine each morning. It arrived at school just as or after the first bell rang. And immediately, classes would begin. Once her school day was over, her bus was the first to leave. That prevented her from participating in any after school activities. It seemed that The Child was destined to grow up knowing only her siblings and the few cousins who lived in their sparsely occupied mountain enclave.

One day, just as classes were changing and as just as The Child entered the classroom, but before the bell rang, Sharon Jones, greeted her with an effusive smile. Sharon was supposedly related. And, in whichever way that was, The Child wasn't interested in pursuing. With her guard up, she realized that Sharon was up to something. And, whatever it was, The Child wanted no part of it. Her mother had given the local beautician orders to cut her hair short. And, when her mother said, short, it meant "really short". Sharon suddenly exclaimed loudly, something The Child could not bear repeating. As her classmates turned their heads around to stare at The Child, they all began to laugh. The color on the victim's face intensified as if to a meter that had unlimited coinage in it.

Of course, she felt humiliated to be the focus of so much unwanted attention. She took her seat and suddenly, Johnny, the boy sitting in front of her, turned around and whispered, "You know what she's referring to, don't you?"

"No, and I don't care."

Johnny couldn't have known how crushed she was to learn this additional piece of information, so insulting was it. She knew he, in his own way, was trying to explain why it was that everyone was laughing.

They all had televisions. The Child and her family did not. And, that had been the source of Sharon's unkind remark, the one that shamed her. She laid her head down on her desk and tried to muffle her sobs, so embarrassed was she. Johnny had always been kind to her; so, she didn't hold what he'd told her against him. But, by the same token, she was mortified. Now, everyone would know just how poor her family was.

As she lay in bed thinking back on the day, distracted from her prayers, she felt so alone.

She wanted, needed, a friend.

Jackie Davis Allen

Revision

Scanning the scene, I discovered a book
Plastered in high relief, surreal in nature
On the landscape were shadows embedded
Ferociously, in the heart of Main Street

Wailing, a flashing strobe reflected
A stethoscope, and as if it were painted
With dread, throbbing shades of pain's
Malfeasance stained the cover bluish black

Praying the script's demise did not include
Me, I tried to remain incognito
My efforts consigned to playing the part
Of a survivor who overcomes fear

Beating erratically, my heart stopped
A steel door opened as if by magic
Before me, glancing right and left, with hands
Plundering, stood one cloaked in ancient garb

Lying on the table, ready, waiting was my pen
It seemed as if it was a sign for me to start
To live again, and so I chose to pick up where
I left off, and the ink began to flow again

Yearning

The heart longs for communion
With soul's divine creativity
Just as mankind desires companionship
For between the two exists a common thread
Granting license to the poet

The cardinal sings his song
And, the fowl-kingdom, listens or not
Mankind experiences both sorrow and joy
From which his heart sings an aria
Affirming, giving meaning to life

The song of the heart yearns
With deepest desire's desiring
Until daily investment inspires
The music, which satisfies both the poet
And the cardinal's residency

Man's soul yearns for nourishment
For meaningful heartfelt work
Wherein the poet and the cardinal trill
As they discover the uniqueness of their quest
Expressing joy with heart's passionate request

Jackie Davis Allen

The Seasonal Call

With a wistful glance back
At her time on Earth
At her once August-appearance
In hues, shades, yellow
Red, rust, chartreuse, gold

Some purples and browns
She is forced to yield the same
Bereft, mourning the loss of her best
Arms naked, bare, we share
The chill of long frigid nights

Skirting reason behind, leaving
One dreads the moment
When reason like treason bites
When with his frosty breath
He slams his bold and bitter face

Against hers, even as he dares to kiss
Her hesitant and trembling lips
Soon, winter will shower the Earth
With the power of his snowy-white
An exercise of ownership and might

Conscious

Of the curious. In the courtyard.
Costumes of propriety, manners were held
in daring disregard.
A canopy of thoughts occupied the head.
Some intensity inflamed.
Abundance of colors, ruby red,
flashed the harsh night.
Like falling clay pots. Subjects, suspects,
forced unwillingly into drawing lots.
Instigated he, the truth.
Despite risking cost.
Propped-up paintings appeared,
as if to clear secret meanings,
to insure the artist of consciousness.
Searching beneath the veneer,
Deciphered then, he, the day,
the visions, the images.
In non-subterfuge ways.
And, so it was, and as if to distill,
the color of truth increased against that
which one might be obligated to pay.
He praying for the innocence of memory, of life
that others, much demented, so wanted to destroy.

Jackie Davis Allen

The Unspeakable

As judge and jury over my own body, I early decided that, if I had done something wrong, I would cry when punished. The converse was also true. If I believed I was being punished unfairly, then, no matter how painful the inflictions to my body, I would not cry.

Still, there was that particular day when, my mother, again, refused to speak to me. It was not right that a mother refused to speak to her child, and especially to one, me, who was abjectly apologetic and wanting to be forgiven.

So, Momma went out one day to visit her mother, just a couple of houses out from ours. I just knew that she was leaving so as to avoid being near me. That made it even more difficult for me, because any opportunity to apologize, again, went away with her. My conscious was bothering me greatly. I wondered how I could get back into her good graces again. I knew that Momma had planned on going out to some function, once she returned from my grandparents' house. We lived in the mountains, coal mining-territory, and evening social events were far and few in-between.

Perhaps, Momma was going to the Parent-Teacher Conference at school? Or, maybe she was going to a baby shower or an engagement shower? It was not likely that she was going to a birthday party, but in any case, I seized upon the opportunity to do something nice for my mother. Hanging up in the front of her closet was the dress she planned on wearing. I plugged in the iron and waited for it to heat up. Surprised and pleased, when she saw the effort I had gone to, in pressing the wrinkles out of her dress, she would change her mind about me. She would smile and be my mother again. She might even say, "Thank you, that was awfully nice of you!" And, then, my conscience could rest. Things would be back the way they were supposed to be.

With the first swipe of the iron, Momma's dress, the place where the iron had landed, shrunk, shriveled and burned! There was a huge stinking gaping hole in her dress. Oh, was I in trouble! Panicked is not strong enough a word to describe the state I was in. And, there were no words to describe what I would say to my mother or how she would react once she came home and discovered her scorched beyond-repair-dress.

When Momma came home and saw the burnt nylon that had been her dress, she burst into tears. How she cried! We both cried. And, I begged for a switching or a belting, but still Momma said nothing to me. She just cried. I do not recall if she went on to the function wearing a different dress. I cried and cried. I felt awful. Selfishly, I had attempted to heal my conscience by manipulating my mother's emotions.

The scarred image of Mommas burned dress remains as a vivid reminder of how important it is to forgive one another. And, how difficult a child I must have been.

Anonymous

She found a poem penned long ago
And, thinking to share it, leaving behind
Her coat of apprehension
She submitted the poem to the Editor
Her hands shook as she handed him the pages
She, wondering if she had made a mistake
Amazingly, he read it, and smilingly said,
"We will print it. Just as it is."

No Illusions . . . through the looking glass

The Sad Days of the 1960s

School's over, at least for the day
Riding on the bus, on the way home
Can't wait to take off my saddle shoes
Brown and white, shoe laces too tight

Wrinkles on my swollen feet
Poppa's at work in the mines
Momma's watching TV, resting
I'm tired; my feet hurt too

I'm anxious to find out
What's been happening on the battlefield
Vietnam, the firing, the dying
God help us! Will it ever end?

Momma looks up and says,
"Time to do your homework"
I mumble during the commercial
"Mine's done, did it during study hall
When's supper?" Momma says, "soon",
As her crochet-needle follows a path
In and out with the thread, a doily
Partially finished, sitting in her lap

As the World Turns ends, fades into
The Doctors; now comes the news
The same on all three TV-channels
Young men dying on the battlefield

The volume turned down, so as not to wake
My baby sister, the firing, the screams
As loud as Vietnam, in technicolor
Red and white, and shaking with fear

Jackie Davis Allen

Ping, ping, rings out the gunfire
Down on the ground, journalists, all
This is surreal; the boy's not much older
Than I, or the boyfriend I wish I had

I'm praying, "God, when will it ever stop?"
Whatever is this world coming to?
It's a living nightmare!
Can't anyone figure out how to stop it?

Pinto beans, cornbread, coleslaw, sliced
Tomatoes, the harvest from the garden
Dinner's ready. Momma's exhausted
Seven children, three to eighteen

Clothing outgrown. And, sitting
At the sewing machine
A pack of new needles, sharper
Than the last ones
"What happened at school today?"
"Same as usual", I say. Momma looks away
But I could see on her mind
All the weight of the world

Food, clothing, books, pencils, paper
And charged lunches, and
"Oh, yes, Mrs. Always on My Back
Asked me, everyone in the lunch-line
Hearing what she said,
'When you all going to pay up'
I lowered my eyes, tried not to cry
And I said, sort of whispered,

'Whenever we can', I wanted to die"
Momma would figure it out, God willing
But how, I didn't know
Before I went to bed, I heard her praying

No Illusions . . . *through the looking glass*

Where there's a will, there's a way
So, please God, help me to find the way!
And so, as the daughter, I write and weep
Pouring out my heart, on this scrap of paper

Anonymous

Jackie Davis Allen

Valedictory Address

We, the members of the senior class, stand tonight at the meeting-point of a happy past and an unknown future. Soon, we will face the commencement of life in the world. But graduation time is also a time of farewell. It marks the end of a definite period in our lives, the period of development.

For the majority of us, this is the end of school-life. What our lives are to be and what we are to accomplish in the world will depend largely upon the foundations we have been building during our school years. For the past four years, the influences we have been subjected to have been quietly and subtly molding our character.

Whether we realize it or not, during these years of our school-life, our energies have been directed toward the day of graduation. As we stand now on the threshold of that day, while we are filled with hopes for the future, we also feel regret for the happy years now ending. But no matter how happy they may be, we will never be quite as gay, and certainly, never be quite as responsible as in the period of our careers now coming to a close.

Tonight, is our only opportunity to say a fond farewell to the friends and advisers who have so dutifully instructed and guarded us all these years. It is also our opportunity to thank them for the many kind words and favors we have so often received from them. So, as we step through the gateway of life, dear classmates, let us say farewell to those who have labored so long and so ardently to teach us how to live; and as we part, let us pledge ourselves to forever remember all the true and lofty ideals which have been born in us here; and to make our lives such to bring fame to our school and cause our instructors to be proud of the class they have so diligently trained for life.

Teachers, do not believe when we speak our regrets at parting that they are but a mere form of words. Do not believe that no feeling animates our speech. Whatever we have gained, be it much or little, and our vanity makes us think it much, we have gained through your care, your teaching, and your apt modes of instruction. We should be base indeed to forget that or forget you. But while you remain at your post of duty, and we get replaced by new pupils, we will march forth from this place, part with the scenes and acts of years, and henceforth, we will become our own commander. We have to speak it under the challenge of the day . . . it is the countersign of the occasion. Ah . . . so hard to utter! Dear principal, dear teachers: Farewell!

And, now, last of all, we, seniors must part in the very hour of victory. We have stood together so long that we have become one body. To sever us is like tearing apart some living thing. What words can express our emotions as we stand here as one for the very last time? Words fail us. So, let us not say farewell to each other. Let us, then, give our farewell to the teachers, to our fellow students that we leave behind. And, to all in this kind audience, who have given us their smiles and good wishes tonight. Farewell!

Jackie Davis Allen

Off to College

Early in my childhood, I learned there was a price to pay for rebelling. All too often, I was willing to pay the price of my parent's disapproval and the resulting corporal punishment, if it meant that I had done something that I should have been given permission to do in the first place.

I became confused when I saw the way that some adults behaved. And, all too often, when I knew what was right and that having acted on that "right," I was punished just as much as if I had done something terribly wrong. Like visiting my grandparents without permission.

I carried the consequences of my actions physically, morally, and emotionally, intellectually, packing them away in the recesses of my being. I was an injured child, hoping to find a way to reconcile these secrets, wrongs, injuries, and hurts into a gift of forgiveness and healing. I talked to God a lot but too often after the fact. I was a mess. A teen-aged compartmentalized mess. I acted like no one, other than God, cared about how I actually felt.

It was on a Friday afternoon that I was sitting cross-legged on the floor in the bedroom that I shared with four of my sisters. Before me sat the trunk. Although, not completely packed, it held the hopes and dreams of my parents. And, especially those of my mother for me. *Where's there's a will, there's a way, and I'm going to find a way for you to go to college.*

I was to finish packing the trunk and have it ready for my uncle to take to the bus station the next morning. It would not fit in our car. But it'd be sent on its way once it arrived at the Greyhound Bus Station in town. My parents were taking me to college the next morning and, for the life of me, I could not believe that it was actually happening. I did not have enough money to pay the balance between what I owed to separate scholarships that were rewarded to me. I was nervous, scared.

I had graduated first in my class. I had my college

acceptance letter in my first-ever pocket-book, a graduation gift from one of Momma's first cousins who lived out west. The letter clearly stated that I was to arrive on Monday at nine a.m. I was to bring with me the acceptance letter and the balance of the year's tuition.

    Momma was happy as a lark, with a crazy smile on her face as if she was singing even though she was not saying one word. Wherever was I to get the money? The State Teacher's Scholarship, with which I was awarded, I would have to either pay it back once I graduated from college, or teach one year for each year's scholarship received. Additionally, I had a State Rehabilitation Scholarship that would provide me with money for textbooks. But more than that amount was due for housing and food. Yet, all I had been given for the trip to college tomorrow morning was two dollars. Yes, you read that right, two dollars.

    The room was hot and little air was moving through the screened-in-windows. Fly-paper, sticky-tapes, hung throughout the house and on the front and back porch. The captured flies were unable to do anything about their predicament. Anxious, I felt trapped, too.

"Momma, you do not understand. My acceptance letter says for me to arrive at nine a.m. on Monday. Not on Saturday morning."

Did she not understand what I was saying?

Momma looked at me and smiled.

"Get back to your packing. You know your uncle needs to have the trunk in his car tonight. That way, when he leaves for work tomorrow morning he won't be delayed. Your trunk will probably already be delivered to the bus station down below the college by the time we get there. We'll take you to the bus station, and we can check to make sure it's there."

I knew the bus station at college was only a few blocks away from my dormitory, but arriving on the wrong day was causing me an intense concern.

"Momma, the letter says the college is closed until Monday. You cannot just take me there on a Saturday and leave me!"

I was nervous and afraid.

"Surely, there will be someone there to let you in. Now, get going and finish up so your Poppa can take the trunk out to your uncle's car. Your Poppa has to work Saturday afternoon and he can't take Monday off from work. We'll be leaving bright and early tomorrow morning."

All day I had been a complete mess, sobbing, and visibly depressed. And, at the same time, I was trying not to upset my mother, who, honestly and truly, seemed unflappable by the obstacles before us. Momma walked back into the living room. And, saying nothing about the lack of progress, evidenced by all the stuff still sitting on my bed and on the floor and the half empty trunk as witness, she cheerfully called out to me.

"There's someone here to see you."

In walked the Big Bad Wolf to my Little Red Riding Hood in an elementary school production. I had not seen him in years, recalling that he had lived with his grandmother the year he and I had been in the fourth grade. Was I ever surprised to see him! We chatted like no time had ever passed. I told him about my situation, about the dilemma I found myself in.

No Illusions . . . *through the looking glass*

After he left, I finished packing my trunk. College was miles away, over narrow and mountainous roads. I should have been excited, instead, I was worried. There was no way my parents or I could have anticipated what was to happen the next morning as we were on our way.

We were to find ourselves caught up in a situation worthy of being featured in a *Believe It or Not* headline.

Epilogue

about the Author

Jacqueline Davis Allen, otherwise known as Jackie Davis Allen grew up in Southwest Virginia, in the Cumberland Mountains of Appalachia. A graduate of Radford University, she makes her home in northern Virginia with her husband, Raymond Gardner Allen. They enjoy spending time at Wintergreen Resort where she enjoys writing while her husband golfs.

No Illusions is the author's third book, different in many ways from her first, *Looking for Rainbows, Poetry, Prose and Art*, and her second, *Dark Side of the Moon*. However, with each book, she has given you a part of the gift with which God has graciously endowed her.

In the past, Jackie has dabbled in antiques, painting, as well as creating soft-sculptured rag dolls. She also designed and made christening gowns for infants. Prior to those creative undertakings, she taught elementary school-age children, both in public and private schools. She has also taught children's art, both in her home and in a commercial setting.

Today, she is happiest when she is writing, although she has not given up thoughts of getting back to her art, even as she is busily at work on her next book.

Other Books

by the

Author

looking for Rainbows

Color Edition

Poetry, Prose & Art

by

Jackie Davis Allen

What Others Are Saying . . .

Jackie is an extraordinary writer. Her work is stupendous. Every page in her *No Illusions. Through the Looking Glass* will leave you wanting more, and I would recommend Jackie's books to anyone who wants to read something remarkable.

Elizabeth Stacy
Grundy, Virginia

Before giving a copy of Jackie's second book, *Dark Side of the Moon*, to my 100-year old mother in Toledo, Ohio, I intended to highlight my favorite poems in the book for her. However, I found that in a second reading for that purpose, every selection once again touched me for different reasons. I felt amusement, encouragement, sadness, joy and lots of bittersweet nostalgia for the past time and places I visited through the plethora of subjects offered in the poems woven by words from Jackie's heart and soul.

Joan Dineen
Springfield, Virginia

Congratulations on your third book, and thank you for the honor to comment on your writings, Jackie! Your work goes straight to the soul. You have an uncanny talent and the ability to say with words what we, as readers, can only feel. Each of your books should be a recommended reading in all healing facilities and on all creative writing arenas.

Deborah Branham
Haysi, Virginia

Reader, the book in your hand, *No Illusions. Through the Looking Glass* by Jackie Davis Allen, a prolific versifier, is no illusion of a poetic craftswoman-ship. I am as enamored by her third book as I have been by her first. I believe you will be too.

In this book, Jackie writes about her childhood, her surroundings of the past and present, along with her hopes for the future. I will focus on one piece alone, "And, It Came to Pass", a poetic prose composition I dub a *ballad*. All plaudits that are the attributes of Jackie's other poems in this collection can be collectively ascribed to this one ballad.

"And, It Came to Pass", is a long but concise poem. Poems require a knack of brevity, which she possesses in abundant supply. At one point in this poem, Jackie says, "It was an ancient settled place time forgot". These lines alone conjure up imagery of historical and ancient ruins I so love. I thought these are memories of old times, not unlike precious ruins we excavate to visit and savor. She incited in me such reaction through her words. In the same poem, she says: "Days came as they would". Again, her words reminded me of the potent inevitability of having to live life with no alternatives. These are simple words and phrases, but the placements are judicious.

Jackie tells me a story. In retrospect. I, like a child, hold her hand and let her take me, wherever she goes. I would love to go along if she were to take me.

Charu Gandhi, Poet
Hoffman Estates, Chicago

Your writings are so powerful, Jackie! Each is very imaginative and relatable. Your use of words and pictures are rich and deep with emotion. Keep penning those most impressive words of yours.

Teresa Marrs Burks
Hurley, Virginia

I am honored to say, I have known Jackie personally all my life. And, I knew how incredibly intelligent she is. However, I did not know the extent of her artistic gifts until I started reading her books and viewing her artwork in them. Like her writings, her artwork, too, is breathtaking.

I have to say that the astounding poetry of Jackie Davis Allen takes you into another world. She is blessed with many God-gifted abilities. I would love to be a talented writer and artist as she is. I highly recommend her writing as well as her art (take note of the cover, which she painted during the Vietnam War). Thank you, Jackie, for blessing us with your exceptional poetic work and your devotion to creating it.

Helen Conrad Justus
Hansonville, Virginia

Beautifully evocative!

Jill Hill
Springfield, Virginia

I was lying in bed one evening, reading Jackie's poetry and trying to calm myself into a sleep. I happened upon the following verse from Jackie's second book, *Dark Side of the Moon*: "Do the rivers of your mind run deep? / Are you haunted by doubts and unable to sleep?" Yes, was my answer. If you have ever felt this way, I highly recommend reading the rest of Jackie's poem, "Dreamscape of the Mind". Jackie has a beautiful way of expressing life's journey.

Geannie Wells
Springfield, Virginia

A great read, brilliant, well-crafted.

Madan Gandhi, Poet
In 2012
Upon reading "Innocence Lost"
By Jackie Davis Allen

I have read many of Jackie Davis Allen's poems. Her themes revolve around human feelings, emotions and experiences. The poems in this third collection, *No Illusions. Through the Looking Glass*, are written in heart's ink. She keeps the reader by her side right from the beginning to the end.

Her poems express the philosophy of life and revolve around profoundly articulated themes. The characters are taken from real life as well as from composite lives, and their emotions are presented in an empathetic tone. Readers can find themselves and many others around them in the characters of her poems, all of whom are embedded in reality. It would be an injustice to the author's talent in crafting prose and poetry not to admire the vividness of her descriptions, pathos and use of metaphors and similes.

Yasmin Khan, Teacher and Poet
Pakistan

Jackie Davis Allen's poetry is elegant and intimate. Reading her work evokes a nuanced picture of captured time, and often relinquishes long-stilled feelings. She has a gift that draws you into her moment. You hear her words and listen to her plea to be present in life, forgive those you have hurt and who have hurt you, and embrace the possibilities within you. In "Fulfillment of a Dream" in her second book, *Dark Side of the Moon*, Jackie writes: "Replaced the blinders in the eyes of those who once placed limits on the blueprint of possibility." She bestows the power within her to inspire us to be all that we can.

Melissa Deutsch
Fairfax Station, Virginia

If asked to name a single person who has influenced me over the years, my answer would be: Jackie Davis Allen. An artist, a poet of mark with a distinct style, an author of two books who has written a foreword to two of my collections, a presence of elitist air, aloof and indifferent, she loves nature. Her literary themes explore complex human relationships with calm and ease. I have known this graceful lady, for very long. Jackie has been both a guide and a valued friend in my arduous journey of discovery, wonder and awe. A poet of consummate ability and superlative genius, her subtle pen dwells deeper into the human suffering and joy.

She excels in story-telling, which is always an account based on reality from the stock of her life. An exclusive genius, she retains her grace and unique style. She has been a great support and an indispensable source of inspiration.

Sadiqullah Khan, Poet
Pakistan

Editor's Notes

No Illusions. Through the Looking Glass is the third extensive book of on which I had the fortune to work together with the author. Jackie Davis Allen's continued confidence in my work is a precious gift to any dedicated editor. Once again, the author presents to those who are closely familiar with her previous literary collections as well as to those who may be reading her creative art in this publication for the first time, a stellar writing – a poetic and prosaic narrative of her unique masterful style. An emphatic stress is called for to note at this point that the final product in your hands had already been crafted by the author with exquisite mastery of all the five language elements. Jackie Davis Allen's sophisticated capability to integrate into a story-telling platform the keen insight she possesses, into the daily life of past and present times, life's out-of-the-ordinary trials and tribulations, self and love, speaks for itself.

With her poetic and prosaic offerings of self-reflective, contemplative, sociologically and personally analytic and all-engaging phenomena, the author invites the reader to a full-fledged interaction with her subject matters. She, thus, rescues the art of writing from the risk it has been facing since the first documented markings of human history – the risk of transpiring as a disengaged voice. Her written art transpires as an intimate exchange. Whether she centers her attention on a theme as common as working on a domestic chore for the family, or on a heart-wrenching experience, such as a parent's agony of losing a child, she waits for the reader with open arms to embrace the emotional or intellectual outcome. In the tradition of her previous books, also in this collection of exquisite writings, Jackie Davis Allen unravels her unique authorial voice yet once again to the awe of her readership.

It is not often that an editor meets a writer who is capable of articulating a large variety of matters of substance in the precise but also eloquent manner as Jackie Davis Allen does. It is, therefore, most appropriate to state here that, from an editorial stance – respectfully excluding the original manuscript's minor oversights in reference to what in the field is called "surface" nuances, *No Illusions. Through the Looking Glass* too, has been a true pleasure to work on. With this note, I extend my thanks to Jackie Davis Allen, a prolific writer, for having given me yet another opportunity to see how upliftingly pleasant an editor's work can be.

hülya n. yılmaz, Ph.D.

Co-Chair and Director of Editing Services,
Inner Child Press International;
Retired Liberal Arts Professor,
The Pennsylvania State University

Links:

innerchildpresseditingservices@gmail.com
https://hulyasfreelancing.com/
https://hulyanyilmaz.com/

a few words from the Publisher

When I think of Jackie Davis Allen and how I am moved and enchanted by the poetic essence of her writing, there is only one way I can summarize its effect upon me:

Telling stories

Graceful is her pen
Lucid memories shared
Tender verse
Touching lines
Careful considerations

She is a weaver of words
Absent of complexities
That lends a movement
To the unsuspecting reader
Who may never be prepared
To be swept away . . .
But we are

I, for one
Willingly will take the journey
With her
As I indulge
In the story-starry, rich lines
Of her poetry
And her prose.

JDA

Inner Child Press

Inner Child Press is a publishing company founded and operated by writers. Our personal publishing experiences provide us an intimate understanding of the sometimes-daunting challenges writers, new and seasoned, may face in the business of publishing and marketing their creative "Written Work".

For more information:

Inner Child Press

www.innerchildpress.com

intouch@innerchildpress.com

www.ingramcontent.com/pod-product-compliance
Lightning Source LLC
Chambersburg PA
CBHW060449170426
43199CB00011B/1144